Charles W. Akers

Abigail Adams

An American Woman

Second Edition

New York San Francisco Boston
London Toronto Sydney Tokyo Singapore Madrid
Mexico City Munich Paris Cape Town Hong Kong Montreal

Executive Editor: Michael Boezi
Managing Editor: Bob Ginsberg
Project Coordination, Text Design, and Electronic Page Makeup:
    Sunflower Publishing Services
Senior Cover Design Manager: Nancy Danahy
Manufacturing Buyer: Roy L. Pickering, Jr.
Printer and Binder: Courier Corporation/Westford
Cover Printer: Coral Graphic Services

Please visit our website at http://www.ablongman.com

ISBN 0-321-32887-6

12345678910—CRW—08070605

To Marcie, Carolyn, and Jeffrey

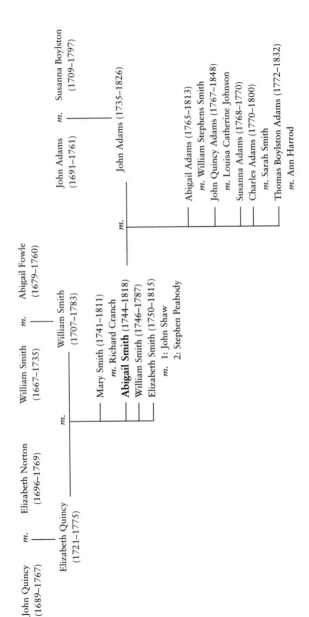

The Family of Abigail Smith Adams
A Selective Genealogy

John Quincy (1689–1767) *m.* Elizabeth Norton (1696–1769)

William Smith (1667–1735) *m.* Abigail Fowle (1679–1760)

John Adams (1691–1761) *m.* Susanna Boylston (1709–1797)

Elizabeth Quincy (1721–1775) *m.* William Smith (1707–1783)

John Adams (1735–1826) *m.*

Mary Smith (1741–1811)
m. Richard Cranch

Abigail Smith (1744–1818)

William Smith (1746–1787)

Elizabeth Smith (1750–1815)
m. 1: John Shaw
2: Stephen Peabody

Abigail Adams (1765–1813)
m. William Stephens Smith

John Quincy Adams (1767–1848)
m. Louisa Catherine Johnson

Susanna Adams (1768–1770)

Charles Adams (1770–1800)
m. Sarah Smith

Thomas Boylston Adams (1772–1832)
m. Ann Harrod

Contents

Preface

As John Adams was caught up in the struggle of the American colonists against Great Britain, he cautioned wife Abigail ro save all of their letters and other documents to show how an ungrateful nation had so shamefully treated their family. She heeded his advice and encouraged their children to do likewise. After four generations, the Adams manuscripts constituted the largest collection of any American family. When grandson Charles Francis Adams published a selection of these in the middle of the nineteenth century, he revealed the richness of some of her keen insights into the issues leading to the Revolution and the formation of the new nation. But not until the 1950's were these papers all opened to scholars to reveal the full Abigail in more than 2,000 letters written by her to many of her contemporaries, both male and female, on both sides of the Atlantic. With an influence unmatched by any American woman of her generation, and as the wife of the second president and mother of the sixth, she deserves the title "First Lady " of the new nation much more than the reticent Martha Washington.

Marriage to John Adams brought his wife a range of experience unequaled by any other American woman of her day, but in that marriage she retained her personal identity and developed into a perceptive, energetic, and intellectually independent person. Her letters provide the fullest personal record of any woman of that period. As far as possible, this book reverses the usual emphasis and try to bring her out from under the shadow of her husband. Events, personalities, and issues will be seen through her eyes, and her ideas are treated for their interest and intrinsic merit rather than as a reflection of John's.

The opening chapter describes what it meant to grow up female in eighteenth-century Massachusetts, and the last offers an overview of her hopes and disappointments on the place of women in the new Republic. Her youthful radicalism on women's rights may have softened with age and parental responsibilities, but not her advocacy of the mutual responsibility of men and women to fulfill their duties in an enlightened relationship. Her concerns for the health and well being of her extended family and neighbors provides a significant chapter in the history of American society.

Charles W. Akers

I

"You May Take Me"

1744–1764

Abigail Adams married a man destined to be a major leader of the American Revolution and the second President of the United States. She gave birth to and nurtured a son who became one of the nation's greatest diplomats and its sixth President. Yet her life did not acquire meaning solely from the glory of these two great men. She was eminently worth knowing for herself. Of all the American women of her time she surely had the widest range of experience, which she recorded in some two thousand extant letters. These discuss the public issues occupying her husband and son, but they also explore the private concerns of women of the Revolutionary generation: the destiny-sealing importance of marriage; the struggle of women denied schooling to educate themselves; the concern for health in an age when physicians often did more harm than good; the meaning of pregnancy and childbirth to mothers; the bonds of sisters and the extended family; the role women were to play in the American Revolution and the new Republic; the relation of religion to the social order; and still more.

The life of this one woman forms a large window on society during the three-quarters of a century that saw the birth and political maturation of the United States. To open this window, and to know Abigail Adams for herself, calls first for attention to those nineteen years of her life during which she was the unschooled daughter of a country minister.

* * *

In 1734, ten years before Abigail's birth, her father had been ordained minister of the North Parish Congregational Church of Weymouth, Massachusetts, fourteen miles southeast of Boston. William Smith descended from a prosperous family of merchants with branches in South Carolina and the West Indies; nevertheless, his parents had pointed him toward Harvard College and the ministry. A patient, gentle youth whose piety was matched by his love of the latest books and slightly risque jokes, Smith took nine years after graduation to complete his studies, settle his religious doubts, and find a satisfactory pulpit. At last he and the Weymouth congregation came to terms, and he took up his duties. Still unmarried, he searched for a wife as carefully as he had for a church, and spent five years finding the right one. In 1739 John Quincy, of the neighboring town of Braintree, consented to the parson's request for his daughter's hand, despite the fourteen years' difference in their ages. After a proper period of preparation, marriage followed in the fall of the next year, and Smith took his young bride home to the parsonage near his meetinghouse.

Elizabeth Quincy came from one of the colony's old and prominent families. The Quincys had been landowners, public officials, and merchants since the early years of Massachusetts. Elizabeth's father inherited lands in Braintree, and on a hill called Mount Wollaston overlooking Boston Harbor built a mansion where he and his wife, the talented daughter of a leading minister, lived a nearly idyllic life for a half century. Close by, his uncle occupied another mansion erected by an earlier Quincy. Braintree's social life centered in these two mansions. With little ambition for greater wealth, Abigail's grandfather devoted himself to public service. During much of his adult life he represented his town in the legislature and was repeatedly elected Speaker of the Massachusetts House of Representatives. In marrying into this branch of the Quincy family, William Smith made for himself and his children a secure place in the major family network of Boston's South Shore.

In the first decade of their marriage, Elizabeth Quincy Smith bore four children: Mary in 1741; Abigail on November 11 (O.S.),* 1744; William (Billy), the only son, two years later; and finally Elizabeth (Betsy) in 1750. Parson Smith joyfully baptized each babe the first Sabbath of its life and dutifully recorded the act in his parish records. The family lived in a comfortable house that he had purchased outright from the congregation to avoid the petty quarrels over use of the parsonage that often plagued New England preachers. When Abigail was sixteen, the father added a wing, larger than the original building, to provide adequate room for children, servants, and the numerous visiting relatives. The Smiths had at least two Negro servants, at first Tom and his wife Peg. Later "Pheebe" appears on the records. These were probably slaves, often called servants in Massachusetts to avoid the dehumanizing connotation of the harsher term. "A negro boy named Cato," purchased in 1761 for £260, was clearly a slave. The size of the enlarged residence, the fine furnishings brought to it by the Quincy bride, and the presence of servants gave

---

*November 22 by the modern Gregorian calendar. When the Julian calendar was replaced in 1752, a correction of eleven days was made.

this parsonage an aura of luxury in the eyes of the common folk in the parish.

Though they lived well, the Smiths had no fortune. By the time Abigail was seven her father made his ministerial rounds in an expensive chaise. Even so, he actively supervised the parsonage farm and another he had acquired north of Boston. Often he labored with his own hands, planting corn and potatoes, gathering hay, sowing barley, or making sure that his many sheep received proper care. His daughters learned to be both household managers and workers. Abigail saw no social stigma in shelling peas with her own hands for a dinner to be served on a table set with fine linen and the best silver.

In a society where marriage and motherhood were the chief functions of every adult female, the relationship to her mother was critical to Abigail's understanding of her identity as a person and of what others demanded of her. Elizabeth Smith mastered to perfection her public role as a minister's wife. She provided work for her poor neighbors, cared for the sick, refused to meddle in the petty quarrels of the parish, and treated everyone with equal affability. Her daughters appreciated her many virtues and talents but looked forward to marriage as liberation from a well-meaning but irksome overprotectiveness. Once Abigail stated the point bluntly: "My Mother makes bugbears some-times, and then seems uneasy because I will not be scared by them." Elizabeth worried especially about her children's health, a worry intensified by her own tendency toward consumption and the fear she might transmit this ailment to her daughters. Abigail long resented being kept home once from a Harvard Commencement be-cause of some "bugbear" about sickness. Since she seemed to catch every disease that came along, she became the special object of maternal watchfulness.

This concern for children's health was under-standable in the light of infant mortality in eigh-teenth-century America. After surviving the per-ilous first year of life, children often fell victim to those dread killers, diphtheria (or throat distem-per) and smallpox. In the great New England epi-demic of 1751 dozens of Weymouth young peo-ple died of the throat distemper, eleven in a single week. The Smith children escaped, and their good fortune continued in the measles epidemic of 1759, when all recovered without the complica-tions that sometimes made this normally mild disease fatal. Best of all, Weymouth missed most of Boston's repeated smallpox infestations, for those who survived this frightful disease might be so hideously scarred as to prefer death. In her old age Abigail remembered that as a young girl she "was always sick." Her ailments were minor but sufficient to start her on a lifetime pursuit of health, a subject about which in time she came to believe she knew as much as most physicians.

Far more than they realized at first, the Smith girls learned from their mother a "patient submission" to their duty in whatever life brought them. Yet they by no means endured a gloomy girlhood. Mary and Abigail—and later Betsy—enjoyed a friendship cemented by harmless little conspiracies against their mother's vigilance. The father's good nature nicely balanced any severity in the other parent. He urged his children "never to speak ill of any Body . . . and to make Things rather than persons the Subjects of Conversation." Abigail was especially close to her Grandmother Quincy, a "merry and chatty" woman bubbling with the latest news, pithy observations on their acquaintances, and pragmatic maxims for successful living. Until her dying day Abigail fondly remembered the long periods she had spent as a child living in this grandmother's house. There were occasional visits to Uncle Isaac Smith. From the handsome home of this Boston merchant and shipowner, the Smith sisters could walk the streets and wharves of New England's largest town, examine the latest styles from London, or attend services at the fashionable Brattle Street Church. Though they lived in separate homes, the various Smith-Quincy families took an active part in raising the offspring of their close relatives.

Weymouth consisted largely of farms and woods. Its widely separated buildings enabled the town to avoid the great fires that heavily damaged Boston from time to time. In 1751 Reverend Smith's meetinghouse burned without the fire spreading, despite the shattering explosion of the town's gunpowder stored in the loft. An improved building replaced it in a few months. Other natural disasters also touched Weymouth lightly. The "great and terrible Earthquake" of 1755 that brought solid brick dwellings crashing down in Boston only shook houses and shattered chimneys in Braintree and Weymouth. The earthquake, though, seemed more ominous because it came at the beginning of the French and Indian War, the American phase of the final struggle between Great Britain and France for control of the North American continent.

Ten years old when the war in America began, Abigail was at an age to sense the crisis of the next five years, when no colonist could be certain of the outcome and many feared defeat. For her, like other young people of this generation, the war years were one long lesson in Christian patriotism. "July 3 [1755]. Fast day on account of the war," wrote her father in his diary. And so it went, year after year: days of prayer, fasting, and sermons to seek divine assistance in preserving the sacred heritage of English Protestant liberty from the French papist foe. A devout participant in these rites who lived to see the miraculous fall of all French Canada to British arms in 1760 could hardly fail to believe that providence supported virtuous nations. When Abigail next saw war, she wrote: "Our Country is as it were a Secondary God."

The religious climate of her home was conducive to the development of such a faith. Her father was one of those clergymen who had softened original Puritanism by accentuating its positive contributions to daily living while neglecting the harsher theological doctrines taken from John Calvin. Since religious authority rested with the local congregation, a minister could move in any direction his people would follow. As a result, almost from the beginning, Massachusetts ministers had developed a variety of religious practices, and in time variations on basic beliefs began to be noticed.

These differences widened during the Great Awakening, the religious revival that swept through New England in the early 1740s. In response to its emotional excesses, William Smith and other ministers who distrusted religious enthusiasm placed greater emphasis than ever on reason and duty in worship. By the middle of the eighteenth century a sprinkling of clergymen no longer taught that Christ was fully divine, that Adam's original sin had corrupted all mankind, or that God saved only a few (His elect) to demonstrate divine mercy. Rather, they maintained the right of every Christian to exercise private judgment on these and other theological points. Two leading Boston churches had ministers holding such views. Nearer home, though Abigail was only nine at the time, she could hardly have missed hearing of the split in her grandfather's Braintree church over its minister's rejection of Calvinism. Grandfather Quincy headed a committee that commended his pastor for promoting a "free and impartial examination into all articles of our holy religion." The center of this liberal Congregationalism south of Boston was the Hingham church of Ebenezer Gay, William Smith's closest friend among the clergy. The two exchanged pulpits frequently.

The liberals nevertheless retained an intense faith: God the Creator had revealed himself to man through the Bible and had given him sufficient reason to discern his moral duty from its pages without the need of human creeds. This benevolent deity rewarded virtue and punished sin, both in this world and the next. Rational re-

ligion was the foundation of morality, the guide
to virtuous living, and the source of freedom. An
irreligious person could not be trusted, and neither could the religious enthusiast whose zeal
blinded his reason. True religion was the only
sure comfort to the afflicted and the one force in
life before which one must bow in total submission. God presided over the destiny of nations
and had some special purpose for the new Christian land the New England fathers had established in America.

Abigail wholeheartedly embraced this faith
when she was admitted to membership in the
Weymouth church in 1759. She took this step,
which climaxed in a public confession of faith,
as she approached her fifteenth birthday. All
three Smith daughters came to their first com-
munion willingly and joyfully. As they grew
older the rational utilitarian religious truth
taught in their father's pulpit became central to
their daily existence. By contrast, brother Billy
did not gain church membership and proved a
major disappointment to the family. He failed to
prepare for Harvard, and his adult life showed a
pattern of irresponsibility and intemperance. As
Abigail later put it, his whole "Life has been one
continued Error"; her father's dying breath was
a prayer for the "reformation and Salvation of
the prodigal." Three bright, pious, dutiful

daughters, and one errant son: the example of her wayward brother was seldom far from her mind as she herself became the mother of sons.

Abigail never went to school. Colonial New England took a casual attitude toward education for females, and many remained illiterate. Some towns did admit girls to the schools that Massachusetts law required them to maintain, yet whatever education young women received generally came at home or occasionally at a private academy in one of the larger towns. Abigail did not go to school because, she later recalled, of poor health. Had she attended she would have learned only enough to make her barely literate, with perhaps a little music or dancing to cultivate the feminine graces.

She mastered the three Rs at home. There was no shortage of teachers: her parents, older sister, and grandparents all served at various times. Yet her instruction remained unsystematic. For instance, she was not taught the rules of punctuation, a deficiency to which she became sensitive in later life. William Smith's library was not large, but he valued books and carefully recorded the titles of those he lent to friends. His mind was open to truth from any source. In addition to histories and books of sermons, he owned a number of modern literary works, among them a complete set of *The Spectator*.

Joseph Addison's essays in this paper published in England early in the century had become models of literary style. His buoyant outlook on life and his advocacy of moral decency and rational religion gave him a wide following in the colonies. Abigail could have found no better primer than the mildly satiric essays of *The Spectator*. Although reading came easily and naturally to the Smith girls as they browsed in their father's study, no one thought to teach them Latin. They were females. French they could learn if they craved the literature of continental Europe; but Latin, the ticket of admission to college and the professions, was reserved for bright young males.

At a critical point in Abigail's education, perhaps as early as her eleventh year, Richard Cranch entered the life of the Weymouth parsonage. Then thirty, Cranch had come from England ten years before. His several technical skills, among them watchmaking, combined with a passion for scholarship. Self-taught, he had mastered the classical languages and a large body of biblical and secular knowledge; and he displayed a pious devotion to rational, broad-minded religion. To top it all, he was a fun-loving companion, and by the time he married Mary Smith in 1762 he had infected the sisters with his zeal for life and literature.

In her sixties Abigail still recalled her debt to this gifted man: "To our dear and venerable Brother Cranch do I attribute my early taste for letters; and for the nurture and cultivation of those qualities which have since afforded me much pleasure and satisfaction. He it was who put proper Bookes into my hands, who taught me to love the Poets and to distinguish their Merrits."

Cranch proved a remarkable teacher. Poetry so filled Abigail's mind that she habitually resorted to it to climax a line of reasoning or express a deeply felt sentiment. Shakespeare, Milton, Pope, and Thomson came first; then she religiously absorbed the new verse of her own day. It was characteristic of her religious orientation that she quoted the poets far more than the Bible. In their graceful rhymes she expressed the divine truths of her faith as well as the pragmatic maxims of her daily life.

Alexander Pope was the favorite poet of the literate young women of Abigail's acquaintance. According to a critical study she later read, Pope was the "great Poet of Reason, the First of Ethical authors in verse"; furthermore, "good sense and judgment were his characteristical excellencies, rather than fancy and invention." His combination of elegance and ethics gave an unforgettable twist to the moral lessons inculcated in the young. Abigail and her friends never tired of quoting such couplets as "True, conscious Honour is to feel no sin, / He's arm'd without that's innocent within."

Abigail's personal favorite was James Thomson, whose long poetical work *The Seasons* was completed shortly before her birth. Pope was a joy, but Thomson mapped the world she knew. As this poet took her through the cycle of changing seasons from spring to winter, he taught her to expect moments of beauty and pleasure but also times of destruction and sadness. Each season brought the potential for human joy, achievement, fulfillment, and renewal, but also the prospect of frustration. For example—as Abigail would so often learn—the long absence of a spouse could deny one the pleasures of the marriage bed, just as the fierce storm could ruin the carefully planted garden. Only in the mind of God did the discordant notes of life blend into a harmonious melody. Thomson offered Abigail the assurance that she could stand amid the opposing forces at each season of her life while still adoring the wisdom and benevolence of a perfect God fully knowable by imperfect man only in the next world.

While Abigail memorized page after page from the English poets, she continued to read whatever prose works came her way. She was particularly taken with the novels of Samuel Richardson, which were still appearing during her youth. To this "master of the human heart," she wrote in old age, "was due whatever I possess[ed] of delicacy of sentiment or refinement of taste in my early and juvenile days." Richardson treated the questions most on the minds of literate, sensitive young women of the eighteenth century: personal identity, duty to family and society, sexuality, marriage, and the role of educated women. Abigail admitted her passion for all his works, even *Pamela* and *Clarissa,* which were intense novels detailing the inner struggles of virtuous women suffering at the hands of lecherous males. In her orderly little world, though, she could sympathize but not identify with Pamela and Clarissa. After suffering with these heroines she took up Richardson's novel of manners, *Sir Charles Grandison,* with relief. The hero of this lengthy work was the "Man of True Honour" whose perfect fulfillment of the varied roles he was called upon to play made his virtue evident. With Sir Charles, virtue was public, not private, and social norms were the standards for measuring character. Until her dying day Abigail defended Richardson against the charge that in Sir Charles he had produced "too perfect a Character." A model should not be flawed, she insisted. She freely applied this standard to the many public characters who were to cross her path, as well as to the men closest to her.

Richardson had high praise for female innocence. He rejected the misogyny (hatred of women) and the misogamy (hatred of marriage) inherited from the tradition of Eve's fall in the Garden of Eden. He celebrated the contribution of a happy marriage to the stability of the family, the basic institution of society. Still he granted the prudent, intelligent woman considerable freedom in choosing a husband. Unless she found a mate of compatible intelligence who would respect her accomplishments, she should be free not to marry, to become a Protestant "nun." Nevertheless, the goal of female education was to produce better wives and mothers. Marriage to such a man as Sir Charles Grandison gave the woman of innocence the sheltered environment necessary for the protection of her virtue and the realization of her full potential. The seven volumes of *Grandison* appeared just before Abigail entered her teens and profoundly influenced her thinking about herself as a woman at the successive stages of her life.

A scarcity of females and the dire shortage of labor in the colonies had temporarily raised the importance of women in America as compared with Europe. The greater functional value of wives and mothers, however, had only slightly increased their economic independence without weakening the theory of a male-dominated society. By the time of Abigail's birth the coastal Massachusetts towns had a surplus of unmarried girls and widows. As a result, few young women could be confident of their matrimonial prospects. This anxiety, stimulated by ideas of romantic love taken from European authors, produced a receptive audience for writings on the institution of marriage and the role of women. Newspapers, sermons, pamphlets, and whole volumes offered advice on this vital subject. Much of this literature pleaded for a proper relationship in the marriage bond: the husband and wife dutifully but lovingly fulfilling their respective roles. As one crude verse in a Boston newspaper began:

> God took not Woman from Man's Head,
> That she should domineer,
> Nor yet out of his Feet that she
> Should all his Burdens bear.

> But near his Heart God did her take,
> A Rib out of his Side,
> To shew that she his loving Mate,
> And half-self should abide.

Most women lacked the options to profit from such advice. But the three daughters of William

Smith understood all too well that their future depended on finding the right husband, their own Sir Charles Grandison. Since there were no vocations suitable for upper-class women, not to marry would leave them economically dependent on relatives. Yet in marriage they would lose their legal identity. As the English jurist William Blackstone explained this relationship, "the very being or legal existence of the woman is suspended during the marriage, or at least is incorporated and consolidated into that of the husband; under whose wing, protection, and cover, she performs everything"— the doctrine of *coverture*. To perform everything for life under the domination of even an otherwise good man who did not share their sensibility to literature would be intellectually stagnating. But even college graduates often wound up as impoverished country preachers, too poor to buy books.

As she neared her seventeenth birthday, Abigail still assumed a half-serious attitude concerning her chances of finding a husband. Responding to a letter from a relative who had just been married, she wrote (in language later polished by her grandson editor): "You bid me tell *one* of my sparks (I think that was the word) to bring me to see you. Why! I believe you think they are as plenty as herrings, when, alas! there is as great a scarcity of them as there is of justice, honesty, prudence, and many other virtues. I've no pretensions to one. . . . I should really rejoice to come and see you, but if I wait till I get a (what did you call 'em?) I fear you'll be blind with age."

A year after writing this letter Abigail saw her sister Mary wed to Richard Cranch. He was thirty-six and the bride twenty-one. This difference in age neither dampened their joy nor lessened the approval of family and friends, for Cranch's learning and gentleness seemed to make him an ideal husband, although his difficulty in earning a living would soon plague his bride. At some point in the festivities the male guests, no doubt warmed with wine, gathered in a room apart from the ladies and began telling "some good Matrimonial stories." One favorite anecdote concerned the bride who had been too frightened to go to bed on her wedding night. Finally, after a long delay, she concluded that "she had put her Hand to the Plow and could not look back." Then, committing her soul to God and her body to the groom, she jumped into bed. The next morning she could not for the life of her remember "what it was that had scared her so."

Five days later one of the guests thought this story worth confiding to his diary. He was John Adams, a twenty-seven-year-old lawyer from Braintree, where his father had been a respected farmer, shoemaker, local official, and church deacon. After graduation from Harvard in 1755, John had disappointed his father by allowing religious doubts to close off the ministry as a career. The young man taught school for a while, then read law until admitted to the bar in 1758. Early marriage, he knew, could ruin an aspiring lawyer. Both he and his close friend Richard Cranch had been infatuated with Hannah Quincy, the flirtatious daughter of Colonel Josiah Quincy and Abigail's second cousin. John came close to proposing once, but someone broke in on them just before the critical moment, and he credited this accident with saving him from "very dangerous shackles" and "absolute Poverty." Now he had settled in Braintree with his widowed mother while seeking a reputation at the law.

John had known Abigail's father at least since the time she was fifteen. At first he considered Parson Smith to be a "crafty designing Man" who hid his wealth from his parishioners, while the two older Smith daughters were witty but shared their father's lack of candor. Nevertheless, John's frequent association with Cranch, Colonel Quincy, and Dr. Cotton Tufts—Abigail's uncle living near the Weymouth parsonage—brought him repeatedly into the company of the family.

By the end of 1761 John had begun to think seriously of Abigail, and their courtship grew warm during the following year. He, of course, had been brought up to think that "the Principal Design of a young Lady from her Birth to her Marriage, [was] to procure and prepare herself for a worthy Companion in Life." Still, he had never met a woman like Abigail, who at seventeen was in his eyes "a constant feast. . . . Prudent, modest, delicate, soft, sensible, obliging, active," and—with all this—physically passionate. A quarter century later she still remembered her thrill and blush when their hands first touched. For his part, he complained that he had given two or three million kisses for each received from her. Despite her religious upbringing, Abigail remained a highly spirited young woman who perhaps deserved the repeated warnings of a neighbor: "Nabby you will either make a very bad, or a very good woman." She long remembered their courtship as a period when emotions pushed hard against the bounds of prudence.

Later generations of Adamses treasured the tradition that the Smith-Quincy families considered John an unworthy suitor because his family was at best of middling quality and the law was a disreputable profession. The story of "what a dance he led" became a cherished legend after the family's rise to fame. Yet Parson Smith recognized John's qualities from the beginning. His wife's hesitation was characteristic of her maternal overcaution and provided whatever substance there was to the tradition. Marriage to one of the Smith daughters brought a good family name, a dowry of household goods, a moderate cash gift, and the distant prospect of inheriting some land. But Mary, Abigail, and Betsy had not been besieged by suitors. Their educational accomplishments were too awesome for well-off young men seeking traditional wives. They had to wait for men who appreciated their minds. As he neared thirty John was ready to take a wife, but the advantages of marrying into this family were insignificant in comparison to what he had found in Abigail herself. Without stepping out of her place as a woman she commanded his intellectual as well as personal respect. Before long they both knew that theirs would be a union of mutual esteem.

In the fall of 1763 Abigail accompanied John on a journey of several days, possibly to attend a court session. By winter they were trying to fix a wedding date. They abandoned thoughts of a spring or summer marriage when the smallpox broke out in Boston. Anyone who traveled as much as John was likely to contract the disease, so he made the difficult decision to be inoculated. His inoculation produced only the mildest symptoms; being away from "Miss

Adorable" for five weeks proved more painful. During this separation, she wrote without restraint, even while acknowledging that she feared him as a critic of her ideas "more than any other person on Earth." But she quickly added that she feared him in no other capacity and never would. And then she asked him to applaud this declaration of fearlessness: "Courage is a laudable, a Glorious Virtue in your Sex, why not in mine?" He facetiously took advantage of her respect for his critical ability by offering to analyze her faults and submitted a list that subtly expressed his admiration for her unladylike "Habit of Reading, Writing and Thinking."

With a fall wedding set, John went off on the court circuit while Abigail made plans for housekeeping. They would live in the saltbox house in Braintree that John had inherited from his father. It stood only a few yards from a similar cottage where John had lived with his mother. In September John still searched for a maid for his wife-to-be. His mother had not been altogether happy with their plans. To please her they agreed to take temporarily the unsatisfactory servant girl she would not need for the winter.

Early in October Abigail was at her Uncle Smith's in Boston to assemble her trousseau. John sent a cart that brought most of her goods to Braintree, after which she wrote him that the remainder would be ready when he returned in a few days from his current court session. "And— then Sir," she added, "if you please you may take me."

II

"An Important Trust"

1764–1774

Abigail and John were married in the Weymouth parsonage on October 25, 1764, a month before her twentieth birthday. She was undoubtedly a virgin; he gave assurances that, despite his twenty-nine years, he was also. Their stored-up passion burst loose and she became pregnant at once. The sudden transition from lover and bride to housewife and expectant mother brought Mrs. Adams a new perspective from which to take the measure of the man she had married.

During a moment of depression on the eve of their marriage, he had frankly stated his expectations of her: ". . . you who have always softened and warmed my Heart, shall restore my Benevolence as well as my Health and Tranquility of mind. You shall polish and refine my sen-

timents of Life and Manners, banish all the
unsocial and ill natured Particles in my Composition, and form me to that happy Temper, that
can reconcile a quick Discernment with a perfect
Candour."

In the decade before he wrote these words,
John Adams had recorded in a diary his inner
struggle to meet the ambitious goals he had set
for himself. While teaching school after graduation from college, he had "resolved not to neglect" his time as he had the year before, but to
strive with all his soul "to be something more"
than persons with fewer advantages. He mused
at the outset of his law career, "Reputation
ought to be the perpetual subject of my
Thoughts, and Aim of my Behaviour. How shall
I gain a Reputation! How shall I Spread an
Opinion of myself as a Lawyer of distinguished
Genius, Learning, and Virtue." A little later he
wrote himself off as "stupid, to the last Degree"
in neglecting to make influential friends. At
twenty-five he believed his life to have been
largely wasted, that it was "high Time for a Reformation both in the Man, and the Lawyer."

But the wife saw a different person, ambitious,
to be sure, yet a man of action rather than a tor-
tured diarist. He was close to the earth, the cultivation of the forty inherited acres never far from
his mind. He directed the hired farmhands and

when home worked in the fields himself. Most of all, she saw the successful lawyer. His practice now flourished; he had as many cases as he could handle. John Adams had stopped keeping his diary more than a year before he married. When he began again three months after the wedding, he had left his pregnant wife in Braintree to attend the January session of the Boston court. There he and a small group of the best lawyers organized a "Law Clubb" from which he anticipated and received the "greatest Pleasure." In the diary he appears confident, relaxed, and sociable. He had found in marriage what he expected.

For her part, Mrs. Adams enjoyed being out from under the watchful eye of her mother, but at times felt an acute loneliness, especially for her sisters. Her husband traveled to court sessions in all but one of the months of her pregnancy. She was not alone; there was a servant or two, and her mother-in-law lived only a few steps away. Yet John's frequent absences cut her off from compatible intellectual fellowship for considerable periods, and most completely when winter snows blocked the road to family and friends in Weymouth. During July 1765 John had court dates in Plymouth and Boston and, as a result, may have missed the birth of his daughter, born a few weeks prematurely on the hot Sunday morning of July 14.

Abigail left no detailed accounts of the births of her children, except the last. Though child-bearing was the main preoccupation of colonial women from marriage to menopause, it remained their private province. The clergy instructed women to suffer silently the curse of Eve and to prepare their souls during each pregnancy for the very real possibility of a childbed death. Female midwives supervised deliveries, while women of the family and neighborhood gathered to offer encouragement. A very few colonial physicians, like Dr. Thomas Bulfinch of Boston, had received obstetrical training in Europe and might assist in life-threatening emergencies. But the sympathetic support of other women remained the chief solace to the mother in delivery. Dr. Cotton Tufts of Weymouth, Abigail's physician uncle, noted the births of her children in his diary as casually as he noted the weather for the day. Like other men, he took childbirth for granted.

Abigail remained home to await the birth of her first child, with her mother and John's on hand to assist the midwife. Parson Smith had exchanged pulpits for this week so he could baptize his granddaughter as "Abigail" in the Braintree meeting house. He recorded the baptism in his diary along with his sermon topic, the birth of Jesus. Her previous susceptibility to disease made Abigail's first pregnancy unusually perilous, particularly after delivery, when childbed fevers often killed a weakened new mother. The general rule was a confinement of as long as a month, during which the mother was constantly guarded against catching cold. Abigail's health interfered with her nursing at least some of her babies. She later wrote that twice her life "was nearly sacrificed to it."

Her sudden pregnancy had dampened the joys of Abigail's first year of marriage. But in the second year the "tender feelings of a parent" erased any disappointments. She was blessed, she wrote to a friend, "with a charming Girl whose pretty Smiles already delight my Heart, who is the Dear Image of her still Dearer Pappa." After both she and Nabby (as baby Abigail was called) recovered from the whooping cough in the spring of 1766, her health was never better. Mentally, however, she suffered from loneliness for her sisters, particularly Mary, who had moved to Salem, a considerable journey north of Boston. Twice, in August and November, John took his wife to visit the Cranch home.

On one of these visits, John and Abigail sat for their portraits by a local artist. These pastel likenesses provide the earliest glimpse of the couple. A twentieth-century historian, Bernard Bailyn, was struck by the contrast between the faces. He saw John's as a "likable but unimpressive face: round, rather soft-looking, bland, and withdrawn . . . with no decisive lines or distinguishing feature." But Abigail's was "extraordinary . . . for the maturity and power of personality it expresses" and was marked by "brilliant, piercing, wide-spaced eyes." It was, Bailyn concluded, "about as confident, controlled, and commanding a face as a woman can have and still remain feminine." Later portraits show the same facial characteristics, most noticeably the penetrating, resolute look of the eyes.

The low neckline of her lace-trimmed dress, the three strands of pearls around the neck, and the swept-back hairstyle of the 1766 portrait reveal that this daughter of Elizabeth Quincy was no stranger to feminine fashion. Her husband observed that during their visit to Salem he for a while had nothing better to do than listen to the "Ladies talk about Ribbon, Catgut and Paris net, Riding hoods, Cloth, Silk and Lace."

In the fall of 1766 Abigail knew that she was again pregnant. Despite frequent visits to Weymouth, an abundance of company, and now four servants, she still felt very much alone during the absences of her husband. She turned to books for guidance and comfort. During this winter of her second pregnancy she read the two volumes of *Sermons to Young Women,* recently published by

James Fordyce, a renowned Presbyterian preacher of London. "I cannot say how much I admire them," she exclaimed to her sister. In this series of sermons she found a complete handbook of the genteel Christian femininity she had taken as the pattern for her life.

Fordyce acknowledged most of the traditionally accepted differences between the sexes. God had created woman to be a helpmate to the man on whom she depended for protection and support. It was accordingly unnatural and impractical for them to exchange roles and thus thwart the divine division of labor. The weaker sex must "allow that war, commerce, politics, exercises of strength and dexterity, abstract philosophy, the abstruser sciences, and the like, are most properly the province of men." A woman should be modest and reserved, recognizing that her "easy elegance of speech" was no substitute for the deeper if less articulate thought of men. Aware of her sexual appeal to males, she must particularly guard against her own inherent susceptibility to flattery. A double moral standard was unavoidable, for in their daily activities men were subject to temptations from which women were shielded. Thus wives and mothers bore the larger responsibility for the preservation of religion and virtue.

Yet Fordyce went on to plead with young women to achieve the full potential of their state. He urged genteel wives to become active managers ("oeconomists") of their households and to perfect their artistic talents in advanced needlework, drawing, and music. He even permitted a "moderate and discreet use of dancing." Though he recommended frugality, simplicity, and modesty in dress as a rule, he acknowledged that in some stations and circumstances splendor was "perfectly allowable, nay exceedingly proper," for women should "avail themselves of every decent attraction."

Furthermore, "the best standard" of her sex required a genteel young woman to make a diligent and proper use of her intellect. Though the female mind, like the body, had been formed with "less vigour" than the male, intellectual accomplishments were still essential. Fordyce prescribed extensive reading, with serious works of history, biography, and travel replacing "Profligate" and "Improper Books." He praised some of Abigail's favorite authors, particularly acknowledging women's great debt to the "incomparable pen" of Richardson. He reminded his young readers that after their girlish bloom had faded the power of intellect would remain. For example, Madame de Maintenon, the last mistress of Louis XIV, had first attracted this most powerful monarch of Europe by the "extraordinary spirit and elegance of her letters." The Presbyterian preacher had nothing good to say about existing schools for girls; instead he urged his "beloved sisters" to educate themselves by reading alone or in small circles: "How smoothly have I seen these hours steal away, which were thus employed in a little ring of intelligent females, all sweetly solicitous to improve and be improved by each other!"

Fordyce's *Sermons* touched Abigail's life at point after point, even to his joining Christianity with the "grand principles of Natural Religion" and stressing morality rather than theology. She read the *Sermons* with one child at her knee and another in her womb, with a husband frequently absent, and with a growing household and farm whose management increasingly fell on her. At some point in her married life, perhaps this early, she reached a fuller understanding of who she was. Born female, she accepted the current view of her nature and the role consequently assigned her. But for this wife and mother such acceptance became a challenge. She resolved to excel in the sphere of life to which femaleness limited her. A modest recognition of her own abilities, together with an understanding of the importance men like Fordyce placed on enlightened womanhood, gave Abigail Adams a strong sense of personal worth that seldom failed her in the many unexpected turns of her life.

Abigail perfectly illustrated this concept of the feminine role in a correspondence with her cousin Isaac Smith, Jr., who visited England in the early 1770s. Though he was only slightly younger, she lectured him on the moral dangers of foreign travel and charged him to report whatever he saw that would "instruct." She acknowledged that "had nature formed me of the other Sex, I should certainly have been a rover." Then she continued in a regretful but proud tone: "Women you know Sir are considered as Domestick Beings, and altho they inherit an Eaquel Share of curiosity with the other Sex, yet but few are hardy eno' to venture abroad, and explore the amaizing variety of distant Lands. The Natural tenderness and Delicacy of our Constitutions, added to the many Dangers we are subject too from your Sex, renders it almost imposible for a Single Lady to travel without injury to her character. . . . To your Sex we are most of us indebted for all the knowledg we acquire of Distant lands."

Here was woman the preserver of virtue and conscious of her supposed limitations, but also insistent that sex roles be fully reciprocal, that men be as accountable for their obligations as women for theirs. Even so, this woman could not suppress her desire to learn about the few females who had stepped out of their place. She urged her young cousin to discover all he could concerning what had prompted Mrs. Catharine Macaulay, the English historian, "to engage in a Study never before Exibited to the publick by one of her own Sex and Country."

The early letters of her married years first made evident the effects of her epistolary style. Eighteenth-century letter writing was a literary art. Richardson, whom Abigail regarded as the greatest teacher of this art, cast long novels into a series of letters; newspaper editors filled their columns with communications from readers; and volumes of correspondence came from the presses. Abigail Adams had since her teens corresponded with a small group of friends and relatives. For most of her adult life she wrote almost daily. Unlike her husband, she kept no lengthy diary in which to record private thoughts. Letters, written in what she described as her "untutored Stile," were her one literary genre.

An epistolary style shaped perception subtly but consequentially. Knowing that there were letters to be written, Abigail tended to organize experience according to interesting highlights, to turn random events into a connected narrative, to judge human behavior according to some eternal truth bolstered by quotations from literary or religious figures, and to put the best possible face on her own conduct and motives. The habitual practice of condensing the complica-tions of life into words that seldom filled more than four pages had a cumulative effect on Abigail, who saw the events of today through the lens of yesterday's letter. Her epistolary style would be most noticeable in later judgments on foreign countries and public figures. For now, her letters forced her to commit to paper a perception of her situation as wife and mother drawn from the precepts of religion and literature, and as a result that perception grew clearer and supplied a guide for daily living. Her letters to John and a few close friends became a revealing form of self-analysis. As she explained once to her absent husband, "My pen is always freer than my tongue. I have wrote many things to you that I suppose I never could have talk'd." During the long years of separation from John that lay ahead, her letters would become even more a form of therapy.

As the birth of her second child neared, Abigail Adams was saddened by news that her beloved grandfather, John Quincy, had taken to his deathbed at Mount Wollaston. She delivered a healthy boy on July 11, 1767. At the suggestion of her mother, he was baptized John Quincy Adams, after the aged man who had died two days following the birth. This baby joined the Quincy and Adams families in name as well as in blood.

Mrs. Adams could now see in her husband the first flush of what she would in time know to be his ruling passion. Far more than by a drive for material success, he was spurred by a quest for fame. In the eighteenth century fame denoted the qualities of greatness: the approval of disinterested public service by fellow citizens, sacrifice for the common good, the ability to shape history, and finally immortality issuing from the approbation of posterity. John Adams could neither seek nor refuse public office. Already he had answered his town's call to serve in several capacities. As tensions between Great Britain and her colonies increased, he found a greater challenge in defending the interests of Massachusetts. His pseudonymous essays on constitutional questions in the *Boston Gazette* had established his reputation among the leaders of resistance to British imperial innovations. No one at the beginning of 1768 could have predicted the opportunities for statesmanship that lay ahead. Yet surely his wife sensed now that the lawyer she had married four years before could never find fulfillment in merely a successful career at the bar. He craved a lifework, he admitted to his diary, that would be like the concentric circles spreading from a small stone dropped in a lake: "Friend, Parent, Neighbour, first does it embrace, our Country next and next all human Race."

To be nearer his important clients and the center of political action, John Adams moved his family to Boston at the end of April 1768. They rented the "white House" in Brattle Square, a choice location in the center of this thriving town. Six times as large as Braintree, Boston crowded its sixteen thousand residents onto a small peninsula. From Brattle Square Abigail Adams looked down to the waterfront and the ships lining the Long Wharf a third of a mile into the harbor. She read the four weekly newspapers as they came from the presses on Monday or Thursday, without waiting for someone to carry them to Braintree days or weeks late. And she diverted herself in the many shops when not busy with family or social affairs. Here too, she observed at firsthand the town's mobs—made up of sailors, young boys, slaves, and even some middle-class citizens—which had become a political force since the Stamp Act riots of 1765. On Sundays she sat in a pew at the Brattle Street Church surrounded by many of Boston's wealthiest families, chief among them the Hancocks and Bowdoins. After the ungainly pulpit manners of her Braintree pastor, Anthony Wibird, she delighted in the eloquent Brattle Street minister, Dr. Samuel Cooper, who, it was said, charmed souls into heaven. Living in this "Noisy Buisy Town" was stimulating.

Still, these years in Boston threw a heavy burden on the wife and mother. Twice the family moved to other houses, with all the resulting disruption. More serious, she bore two children in rapid succession. A sickly daughter, Susanna, born at the end of 1768, died thirteen months later. Consumed with sorrow, Abigail wrote few letters in this period. Her husband of necessity rode the court circuits as usual, yet he realized the load of anxiety she carried. He long remembered that on the evening of the Boston Massacre (March 5, 1770) he had rushed home past soldiers with fixed bayonets to calm the fears of his pregnant wife. A second son, named Charles, was born at the end of May 1770.

Depressed with the turn of public affairs and suffering serious fatigue from the demands on his time, John Adams sent his enlarged family back to Braintree in April 1771, while he kept his law office in Boston. Country air, horseback rides from home to office, and a trip to mineral springs in Connecticut revived his health and spirits. One result of this period of renewal was the birth of a third son, Thomas Boylston, in September 1772. Abigail and John may have agreed that four living children made a sufficient family. In any case—and by whatever means—she went five years without another pregnancy. Much later, she acknowledged that she did not hold to the fatalistic belief that a wife must have all the children that came her way. But the subject of birth control was too delicate for her to be more specific.

All his protestations to the contrary, John Adams could no more retire from public affairs than he could stop breathing. In August 1772 he purchased a substantial brick house in Boston, to which he moved his family in late November. While her husband served his clients and stood guard on the royal government, Mrs. Adams grew increasingly concerned over the responsibility of rearing her four children. Nabby, now seven, and John Quincy at five were ready for serious learning, and the two younger sons seemed not far behind. All her reading stressed the responsibility of the mother in shaping the mind and character of the "tender twigs" entrusted to her care by providence. "I am sensible I have an important trust committed to me," she wrote; "and tho I feel my-self very uneaquel to it, tis still incumbent upon me to discharge it in the best manner I am capable of."

Abigail's concern for her methods of child rearing increased during a visit in the summer of 1773 to the home of Mercy Otis Warren in Plymouth. Mercy was a daughter of the powerful Otis family of Barnstable. Her brother James had with his pen and oratory led the fight against royal government. Married to the important Plymouth farmer-politician James Warren, Mercy Otis aspired to a literary career even while giving birth to five sons, and by the time of Abigail's visit had written poetry and published her first political satire in a Boston newspaper. The trip to Plymouth marked the commencement of a long friendship and correspondence between the two women. At first Abigail was somewhat overawed by her new friend, sixteen years older than she, and even made a few unfortunate attempts to imitate Mrs. Warren's artificial literary style. They were kindred souls, though, who in their small private worlds exerted the full strength of well-furnished intellects. Both loved books, and Abigail's direct access to the Boston booksellers gave her at least one advantage. She surely understood, though, that Mrs. Warren longed to have successful men recognize her genius. Letter after letter from Plymouth contained none too subtle hints that the opinion of John Adams mattered more than his wife's. At twenty-eight, Abigail did not resent this attitude as much as she would later.

Most of all, the days she spent at Plymouth left Mrs. Adams impressed with the "happy fruits" of the "well ordered" Warren family. With her sons gathered about her for instruction, the self-assured, articulate Mercy Otis Warren was indeed an unforgettable sight. But when Abigail asked for advice on child raising, she received little but an acknowledgment that the "discharge of a duty that is of the utmost importance to society . . . for a Number of Years . . . is almost wholly left to our uninstructed sex." Here was the major argument that literate mothers of the Revolutionary generation advanced for the schooling of their daughters: society placed the heavy burden of early childhood training on mothers who as girls received little or no education. This issue became more poignant after the American Revolution, when the strength of the republic was equated with the virtue of each new generation. Yet already, the mother of the four children of John Adams sought to bring them up not only to "do honour to their parents" but also to prove a blessing "to the riseing generation." When one of the Warren boys proved a major disappointment to his parents, Abigail Adams reflected on the possibility of failure with her own children. Nor could she forget brother Billy, who was slowly sinking into alcoholism and had begun raising children he could not support. In later years John Adams devoted long passages of his letters to the education of their children, but he was seldom home long enough to lift the burden from his wife's shoulders.

Abigail saw John Quincy as a handsome, spirited child whose vitality, like her own, held great potential for either good or evil and thus required careful direction into proper channels. Each day began by reading to the children a chapter from the Bible, a habit the mature John Quincy would continue throughout his life. His first children's book appears to have been *The Renowned History of Giles Gingerbread: A Little Boy who lived upon Learning,* an English publication reprinted in the colonies at about the time of his birth. Little Giles Gingerbread, a dutiful and honest but poor boy, envied the coach of a rich man. His father, a baker, taught Giles that "Merit and Industry may entitle a Man to any Thing." But first it was necessary to learn to read, so the father baked gingerbread books which Giles ate as he mastered each lesson, thus actually living upon learning. As Giles improved his reading, the lessons became more moralistic, combining happiness in this life with preparation for the next. The stories taught the values the mother hoped to inculcate in her children: duty to family and society, unfaltering morality, undogmatic piety, regular industry, and zeal for learning. In later life, as she watched John Quincy's precocious career, one of her fondest memories was his learning the stories from Giles Gingerbread by heart while hardly more than a toddler.

October 25, 1774, marked the tenth wedding anniversary of the Adamses. Abigail was alone, her husband too busy at the First Continental Congress in Philadelphia even to note the occasion. The summer before, the family had moved back to the Braintree farm, which John Adams had enlarged by purchase of his father's homestead. He felt more secure leaving his wife at their farm than in Boston, despite her greater responsibilities there.

If she contemplated what these ten years of marriage had brought, she could hardly have agreed with her grandson, Charles Francis Adams, who later wrote that the first decade of her married life had contained little "worthy of recording." In these years Abigail Adams had discovered who she was and what role she would play. She had adjusted successfully to life with a husband driven by profound anxiety for his future; he not only respected and sought her advice on major matters but thought her capable of carrying out whatever duties he left to her. John and Abigail had achieved in this marriage a friendship and mutual respect that would last a lifetime, a remarkable tribute to her understanding of the possibilities as well as the limits of her place as a woman in a man's world. Five times in ten years she had risked death to bring a child into the world. She had buried one and now felt keenly her duty to raise the others. These were developments which her statesman grandson, eager to move on to great political events, could pass over as commonplace and hardly worth mentioning.

Abigail's sisters understood the primacy of these concerns. The three Smith daughters never ceased to maintain a close relationship based as much on a common feminine outlook as on blood ties. The correspondence of their lifetimes provides remarkable documentation for the importance of sisterhood to eighteenth-century women. Their assistance would enable John now and Abigail later to be away from home frequently and for long periods of time. The three reached maturity nearly equal in education and talents, but their fate in marriage largely determined their adult lives. Mary Cranch was happily married, wanting only to be near Weymouth to make life complete. Leaving Salem, the Cranches resided briefly in Boston, then settled permanently in Braintree, where their lives happily intertwined with the extended family. Even though her husband's watchmaking business never flourished, Mary supplemented their income by taking in boarders, one of the few occupations available to middle-class women; and she made their home a haven for the less fortunate of the neighborhood.

By contrast, on her twenty-fourth birthday Betsy Smith, who at times appeared the brightest of the sisters, remained unmarried and without prospects. In 1774 she wrote to Abigail, "Whenever I find myself laying Plans of future Felicity, I check the career of my Imagination, and consider that much Tribulation is the inevitable Lot of Humanity." She joked that she was becoming the favorite of elderly gentlemen, but it was no laughing matter when Abigail warned her against being too free in her conduct toward a male boarder in the Smith parsonage, a schoolteacher of her own age whom she eventually married. Betsy aggressively defended her warm, open relationship with honorable persons of both sexes: she should not be censored by a sister "Highly favoured among Women" as a result of sharing the confidence and possessing the esteem of a husband like John Adams. In a decade Betsy's sister had forgotten the anxiety of those last few years before the young Braintree lawyer came her way.

The Smith sisters were much more the masters of their destiny than the masses of ordinary women who lived in poverty and ignorance, bearing children with or without marriage and daily laboring at monotonous women's work with little hope of improving their lot. Abigail Adams had useful family connections, a constant supply of literature and the education to read it, servants to carry out routine tasks at her direction, and a prosperous husband willing to accept his wife as an intellectual equal, at least within the confines of the family circle. Still, these advantages had made her only more sensitive to the adjustment society demanded of her as a woman.

III

"Remember the Ladies"

1774–1776

John Adams was no radical screaming for independence from the mother country; but he stood firm against the British ministry's new attempt to tax Americans. For ten years Abigail Adams had watched her husband's increasing absorption in the political and economic issues driving Great Britain and the thirteen colonies apart. They were married in the year that the Sugar Act brought cries of doom from John Adams's merchant clients. Nabby was born at the beginning of the Stamp Act crisis in 1765, to which her father responded with a series of newspaper articles tracing the rise of human freedom in the face of political and religious tyranny. John Quincy's birth came in the year that the Townshend Acts reasserted parliamentary authority over the colonies. The birth of the sickly Susanna in 1768 nearly coincided with the arrival of Redcoats to protect royal officials from Boston mobs. Lawyer Adams, now in the thick of resistance to the mother country, successfully defended John Hancock and James Otis in cases arising from confrontation with the crown. When Charles was born in 1770, John Adams had taken the defense of the soldiers accused of murder in the Boston Massacre in order to demonstrate the colony's concern for impartial justice. Afterwards he represented Boston in the Massachusetts legislature and attacked British policy in the press. By the time Thomas Boylston Adams entered the world in 1772, his father was a leading political figure as well as the preeminent lawyer of Massachusetts.

Mrs. Adams had borne their five children while dutifully supporting her husband's need to accept political responsibility. Elected to the Massachusetts assembly at a critical moment in the resistance movement, he accepted and then went home to pour out his apprehensions to Abigail. As he recalled many years later, "That excellent Lady, who has always encouraged me, burst into a flood of Tears, but said she was very sensible of all the Danger to her and to our Children as well as to me, but she thought I had done as I ought, she was very willing to share in all that was to come and place her trust in Providence."

Abigail Adams could not expect to be more than a private observer and supporter of her husband's public career. The great voices of the European Enlightenment, notwithstanding their attack on established institutions, had almost never challenged the traditional assumption that women stood outside the political process. Likewise, the radical seventeenth-century English republican writers from whom American Whigs drew their political philosophy had concerned themselves with opposition to arbitrary royal power, not with fundamental questions of the social order such as the position of women. When exceptional women, like Catharine Macaulay or Mercy Otis Warren, forced their way into the literary world, they wrote about the activities of men rather than the condition of their own sex. Massachusetts women did not vote, hold office, or even attend town meetings. They existed in the private world of the family; they were domestic creatures who depended on fathers or husbands to represent them in the public sphere. The male was the free individual whom the republican philosophers heralded as the foundation of liberty and virtue. Wives and daughters enjoyed a political existence only in their relationship to men.

Abigail Adams's husband considered her an intellectual equal and enjoyed discussing politics freely with her in the confines of their home. Without asking him to yield any of his male prerogative, she presented herself as the whetstone on which to sharpen his ideas. Her opinions were not merely a mirror image of his; she was often the more incisive and unwavering of the two. She became skilled in striking a fine balance between deference to male superiority and the persuasive presentation of her views. Denied a public voice, she helped shape the political views of her husband and sons. Her aptitude was so great that she gradually enlarged her private political influence through a wide circle of correspondents and acquaintances. She became in time the nation's best informed woman on public affairs, while never overstepping, she thought, the line nature had drawn between the sexes.

This process began before the Revolution. At first too preoccupied with maternal concerns to do more than wonder with amusement at John's overly loud protestations that he cared nothing for politics, by 1770 Abigail was fully aware of his serious involvement in the crisis. Already for her, England had become their "cruel" mother country. When the mature George Whitefield, the disruptive evangelist of the 1740s, came to Boston once more in 1770, Abigail heard him preach a sermon that implied, thanks to the earlier revivals, that the colonies now displayed more genuine religion than hypocritical England. As much as she disliked emotional revivalism, this message increased her pride as an American. Like others, she welcomed the politically quiet period between the Boston Massacre of 1770 and the Tea Party of 1773; but the ideological foundation had been firmly laid in her mind. While Massachusetts awaited its fate after the destruction of the tea, she wrote of the British ministers and their co-conspirators in America, "How unbounded is ambition and what ravages has it made among the human Species. . . . But that Ambition which would establish itself by crimes and agrandize its possessor by the ruin of the State and by the oppression of its Subjects, will most certainly defeat itself."

On August 10, 1774, Abigail parted with John as he left to attend the Congress called at Philadelphia to unite the colonies against Great Britain's plan to punish Boston and Massachusetts. She did not hear from him for five weeks, though she faithfully wrote letters of encouragement. "Your task," she assured him, "is difficult and important. Heaven direct and prosper you." During his absence she developed a "very great fondness" for reading about the classical heroes so often held up as examples by American patriots. The popular volumes of didactic ancient history by the French Jansenist Charles Rollin, available in an English translation, filled her "days of solitude," and she encouraged John Quincy, now nine, to read a page or two aloud to her each day so that he might share the inspiration and lessons of the classical struggle against tyranny.

Though her sons would not be of military age for another decade, Abigail Adams dreaded war, the outcome of which only God knew. Yet she feared more the loss of American freedom if her countrymen purchased peace "at the price of liberty." Opening a correspondence with Catharine Macaulay late in 1774, she wrote that "the only alternative which every american thinks of is Liberty or Death." The colonies did not desire independence unless Britain forced it on them: connected by "Blood, by commerce, by one common language, by one common religion as protestants, and as good and loyal subjects of the same king," they earnestly wished that "the three fold cord of Duty, interest and filial affection" would not snap. "Tis like the Gordean knot. It can never be untied, but the sword may cut it."

When John Adams came home from Philadelphia in November with assurances that most of the colonies would stand with Massachusetts against Britain, the province was in open rebellion. Everyone knew of the British general's preparations for war in Boston. Abigail had witnessed from her open window the seizure of the local powder supply by Braintree patriots fearful lest it fall into royal hands. A Provincial Congress, organized in defiance of the royal governor, had set itself up as the de facto government and in December elected John Adams one of the Massachusetts delegates to the Second Continental Congress, scheduled to convene in May. During the interval he found little law to practice and filled the time by writing a long series of newspaper essays defending American resistance against the challenge of an able loyalist.

Abigail's attitude toward the mother country hardened even while her fears increased. She steeled herself for the coming bloodshed with epistolary bravery: "Is it not better to die the last of British freemen than live the first of British Slaves." After reading that George III had denounced his American subjects at the opening of Parliament, she exclaimed to Mercy Otis Warren, "The die is cast. . . . Heaven only knows what is next to take place but it seems to me the Sword is now our only, yet dreadful alternative."

Then came the first shots of the Revolution at Lexington and Concord on April 19, 1775. A week later delegate Adams was again on his way to the Congress in Philadelphia, leaving his family alone only a half hour's ride from the American lines encircling the British army in Boston. From

Connecticut he sent advice of little comfort. He cautioned Abigail against taking fright at every false alarm, but in case of real danger she should "fly to the Woods" with the children. Mrs. Adams had grown accustomed to caring for the family while her husband pursued his career. But this time there was a war under way, and she had not the slightest idea when or even if he would return.

As she received the "fly to the Woods" advice, there was reason to believe that the Redcoats would attempt an attack by sea on some of the towns surrounding the bay. Every alarm sent minutemen marching past the Adams front door, hungry, thirsty, looking for a sheltered place to rest. Refugees from Boston, permitted to trickle out of that besieged town, sought temporary asylum as they moved south through Braintree. "You can hardly imagine how we live," Abigail informed John a month after his departure.

The shock of war confirmed Abigail's perception of resistance to Britain as a righteous struggle of a free people against arbitrary, enslaving power. She freely expressed her views to a London bookseller: "I glory in calling my self" a daughter of America, she announced. The colonists fought because "Tyranny, oppression and Murder" had been their reward for "all the affection, the veneration and the loyalty" they had given the mother country. "The Spirit that prevails among Men of all degrees, all ages and sex'es is the Spirit of Liberty. . . . Every peasant wears his arms, and flies to them with the uttermost eagerness upon every allarm." More than a year before July 4, 1776, Abigail Adams predicted and declared herself ready to accept independence: "Tis Thought we must now bid a final adieu to Britain, nothing will now appease the Exasperated Americans but the heads of those trators who have subverted the constitution, for the blood of our Breathren crys to us from the Ground."

The intensity of feeling with which Abigail Adams accepted the war sprang in part from her transfer of religious emotion to the colonial political cause. She was as deeply committed to her liberal beliefs as any Puritan had been to Calvinism. Her faith blended easily with the Whig ideology to support a holy war in defense of liberty and property. War was always an appeal to heaven, so even John Locke had acknowledged. Thus, in Abigail's words, "Our Country is as it were a Secondary God, and the first and greatest parent. It is to be perferred to parents, to wives, children, Friends and all things the Gods only excepted." Rollin's histories had confirmed what she already believed: religious and political liberty were inseparable. John Quincy remembered all his life that during the early months of war his mother led him daily in a two-part devotional exercise. First they repeated the Lord's Prayer and then recited the "Ode" by William Collins glorifying the brave warriors who had fallen while suppressing the Jacobite rebellion of 1745. This popular poem began, "How sleep the brave, who sink to rest, / By all their country's wishes blest!"

On June 17 his mother took John Quincy to the top of Penn's Hill near their home to watch the Battle of Bunker Hill. They heard the roar of cannon and saw the flames of burning Charlestown. Soon they learned of the appalling price the British had paid to drive the American troops from hastily erected fortifications. The American losses were lighter in number but costly in quality. Chief among them was their close friend and Boston physician, Dr. Joseph Warren, whose skill in setting a "very bad fracture" had recently saved John Quincy from the loss of a finger. With "bursting Heart," Abigail scribbled the sad news of Dr. Warren's death to John with the comment, "The race is not to the swift, nor the battle to the strong, but the God of Israel is he that giveth strength and power unto his people." An eyewitness to a war that any hour might cross her threshold, she nevertheless found the spiritual resources to cheer a husband safely removed from the fighting: "I think I am very brave upon the whole," she wrote to

Philadelphia. Though she complained that John's letters were too short and cold, she acknowledged, "I must not grumble. I know your time is not yours, nor mine." As if to compensate, hers to him grew longer, filled with details of the war in Massachusetts and of their family and domestic concerns. More than ever, letter writing became a way of life for her.

Abigail Adams fully shared the ecstasy—the "Spirit of '76"—of the first year of the Revolution. In her own neighborhood she noted with pleasure the increased respect paid her as the wife of a Revolutionary leader—"Mrs. Delegate," as she sometimes fancied calling herself. ("Why should we not assume your titles when we give you up our names.") When the generals sent by Congress to command the army at Boston reached the area soon after the Battle of Bunker Hill, they made themselves known to Mrs. Adams. She "was struck by General Washington" and, like many other patriots, instantly saw godlike qualities in him. It was more difficult to accept the eccentric, slovenly General Charles Lee with his pack of dogs, but her patriotism rose to the occasion. This Englishman, now fighting for the colonies, took a strong liking to Mrs. Adams, particularly after her husband had made the general's dogs famous on both sides of the Atlantic. In a letter intercepted by the British and widely published in loyalist and British newspapers, John Adams had written of Lee, "you must love his Dogs if you love him." The first time he met Abigail after the publication of this letter, the general insisted on formally introducing her to his favorite dog. Her patriotism was again severely tested as she accepted the outstretched paw.

For all devout patriots, July 20, 1775, was memorable. Congress had set that date for a day of prayer and fasting throughout the colonies to seek divine aid in the struggle with Britain. So completely did Americans observe the fast that this Thursday became known as "Congress Sunday." It was as if all America had suddenly become New England. Not wanting to hear the dull Braintree preacher on such an important occasion, Abigail and her sister Mary rode eleven miles to keep the fast at Dedham with her "Sister Delegate," the wife of Samuel Adams. She thought it safe to travel because the British were not likely to attack colonists on their knees. "I really believe," she wrote John, "they are more affraid of the Americans prayers than their Swords."

John Adams returned to Massachusetts unannounced on August 10. Before he could surprise his family in Braintree, he was detoured by an urgent request to attend the provincial legislature meeting behind the American lines at Watertown. For the next three weeks Abigail saw him only on weekends and during the three days she spent at Watertown in the last week of August. Then he was off again for Philadelphia. He left behind a major epidemic of dysentery, likely touched off by the poor sanitation practices of American soldiers. This debilitating and often fatal intestinal disease killed one of his brothers and took a heavy toll as it spread through Braintree and Weymouth. Dysentery turned the Adams house into a hospital, with Tommy and several servants laid low. When Abigail herself developed the symptoms—fever, cramps, and bloody stools—it was all she could do to keep from sending after John to return to his sick family. All eventually recovered except a servant girl who slowly wasted away, a horrible sight to behold. Abigail was hardly on her feet again when her mother contracted dysentery, after having disregarded her own health by making daily trips from Weymouth to Braintree to nurse her daughter and grandchildren. Now Abigail in turn became the nurse, spending twelve hours a day in the sickroom for more than two weeks while Elizabeth Quincy Smith rapidly weakened. She died on October 1.

Her mother's sacrificial death left Abigail with deep psychic scars. Like many daughters, she had been unable to understand and appreciate an overwatchful mother until she had raised children of her own. Now the memory of her teenage impatience with maternal restraint turned to remorse as she lovingly recalled Elizabeth Smith's great "care and tenderness" and the final sacrifice of her life to nurse loved ones. Five weeks after the funeral Abigail still spent the quiet hours of each evening thinking of her departed parent. Nearly a year later she admitted to John that the "Image of my Dear Mother seems ever before me, and fresh to my memory," and she continued to suffer depression when entering the Weymouth parsonage to visit her father. Still, she resolved "to submit with christian resignation" to the "Will of Heaven" and to "acknowledg the justice of the Hand that chastises me."

During this period of potential danger and personal grief, Abigail began to reflect more frequently on human nature, which she believed to be the same "in all ages and Countrys." Avarice and selfish ambition were the lot of mankind. No one could be trusted with power who did not sincerely join public patriotism with religious and moral integrity. There was no better example than Dr. Benjamin Church, prominent Boston Whig and chief physician of the Continental Army, who now stood accused of spying for the enemy.

Abigail acknowledged "some pretensions to physiognomy"—the art of judging character from facial features. When the venerable Benjamin

Franklin visited the Boston area in the fall of 1775, she sat down to dinner at her Uncle Quincy's with the renowned philosopher and scientist. She observed his "grave, yet pleasant, and affable" manner, studied his face, and then pronounced Franklin a "true patriot" with "every virtue of a christian."

Abigail reached a different conclusion concerning John Hancock, of whom she stood in no awe. He had grown up in Braintree with her husband and had recently married into the Quincy family. After inheriting the fortune of his Boston uncle, young Hancock had attached his money and reputation to the Whig cause. He had gone as a delegate to the Second Continental Congress and been elected president when the first presiding officer was called home, but did not relinquish the office when his predecessor returned. Abigail saw this refusal to step down as a weakness of Hancock's character: at best this important Boston merchant-politician was vain, at worst morally deficient.

Abigail discovered new significance in her life by the motivation she attributed to the behavior of others. By inferring that Hancock's showy patriotism sprang from vanity or baser motives, she could more confidently interpret her husband's public service and the sacrifices she made to support it as purely disinterested. She insisted that others meet the rigid standards of virtue she believed were needed to establish and preserve a free republic. The personalities of Abigail and John had become more nearly alike than when they were first married. Now she needed to find new meaning for her life fully as much as had the young diarist setting out to study law. In the hundreds of letters between them—again the epistolary style left its mark—they confirmed each other's opinions of their countrymen. Hancock at first, and later Franklin and Hamilton, became their chief psychological foils, but even the normally untouchable Washington served the purpose on occasion, not to mention scores of less significant colleagues. In time, perhaps because hers was a private role, Abigail became even more judgmental than John. But her mind was never closed to new evidence; thus her opinions were not unalterable.

As the winter of 1775–1776 approached, Abigail described herself as a "nun in a cloister," with no social life outside the family. She sensed that her situation would never improve until the colonies had reached the inevitable end of the path along which resistance to Britain had taken them. She wanted independence, and soon: "Let us seperate, they are unworthy to be our Breathren." She scolded John and his fellow delegates for the timid language of their official documents. "Very angry," she insisted that such caution only created a fear of independence in the minds of uninformed people.

John arrived home in December, likely before receiving this chiding. After a week in Braintree he rejoined the legislature in Watertown, which re-elected him to Congress, and the last week of January he set off again for Philadelphia. Seemingly crushed at his brief stay, Abigail waited a month to answer his letters. Her first reply acknowledged receipt of *Common Sense*. She did not yet know this pamphlet to be the work of the English radical Thomas Paine, but she fully appreciated its eloquent argument for independence. Thanking John for it, she wrote, "I have spread it as much as it lay in my power, every one assents to the weighty truths it contains. I wish it could gain Credit enough in your assembly to be carried speadily into Execution." How could any friend of the colonies "hesitate one moment at adopting" the appealing sentiments of *Common Sense?* Quoting Shakespeare's *Julius Caesar* (IV.iii.221–227), she reminded her husband and the Congress that

> There is a tide in the affairs of men,
> Which taken at the flood leads on to fortune;
> Omitted, all the voyage of their life
> Is bound in shallows and in miseries.
> On such a full sea are we now afloat,
> And we must take the current when it serves,
> Or lose our ventures.

During the first days of March, Abigail sensed that some large military endeavor was under way as she listened to three days of intermittent cannon fire and watched the minutemen rush past her front door. She climbed Penn's Hill to see for herself the flight of shells into Boston from the American lines. The bombardment proved to be a cover under which Washington's men placed artillery on the nearly impervious terrain of Dorchester Heights overlooking Boston. After some hesitation the British general realized his impossible plight and gave the order for evacuation. Boston's liberation came on March 17.

With mixed feelings she watched sail away the "largest Fleet ever seen in America." Her elation at this magnificent and nearly bloodless victory was dampened by the thought that "tis only lifting the burden from one shoulder to the other which perhaps is less able or less willing to support it." She had serious doubts that Virginians, for example, could stand against "our common Enemy" as had New Englanders. Except for Washington, she had seen little evidence that the "Lords and common people" of that colony were not "like the uncivilized Natives Brittain represents us to be." Equally serious, Virginians were great slaveholders. Repeated attacks on slavery in the local newspapers during the years preceding the Revolution had pricked Abigail's conscience. While living in Boston she had experienced for herself the threat of an enslaved black people striking out in blind rage against their white oppressors. Consequently, she pondered how Virginians could fight for freedom while denying liberty to nearly half their population: "I have sometimes been ready to think that the passion for Liberty cannot be Eaquelly strong in the Breasts of those who have been accustomed to deprive their fellow Creatures of theirs. Of this I am certain that it is not founded upon that generous and christian principal of doing to others as we would that others should do unto us."

These lines came from Abigail's letter to John of March 31, 1776. After pointing out that slavery was a contradiction to Whig ideology and the Christian religion, she went on to discuss what she hoped would be a major consequence of the independence for which she prayed:

> I long to hear that you have declared an independancy—and by the way in the new Code of Laws which I suppose it will be necessary for you to make I desire you would Remember the Ladies, and be more generous and favourable to them than your ancestors. Do not put such unlimited power into the hands of the Husbands. Remember all Men would be tyrants if they could. If perticuliar care and attention is not paid to the Laidies

we are determined to foment a Rebelion, and will not hold ourselves bound by any Laws in which we have no voice, or Representation.

That your Sex are Naturally Tyrannical is a Truth so thoroughly established as to admit of no dispute, but such of you as wish to be happy willingly give up the harsh title of Master for the more tender and endearing one of Friend. Why then, not put it out of the power of the vicious and the Lawless to use us with cruelty and indignity with impunity. Men of Sense in all Ages abhor those customs which treat us only as the vassals of your Sex. Regard us then as Beings placed by providence under your protection and in immitation of the Supreem Being make use of that power only for our happiness.

These bold paragraphs were not a declaration of the principle of sexual equality for which nineteenth- and twentieth-century feminists would contend. Abigail Adams did not call for a revolution in the roles of men and women. She hoped rather for a legal system under which women could find maximum fulfillment in their ascribed roles as wives and mothers, as domestic beings deferential to, but not abused by, fathers and husbands. Steeped in Whig ideology, she believed that no one could be trusted to exercise "unlimited" power over another, not even a husband over a wife. The recent publication of

William Blackstone's *Commentaries on the Laws of England* had reminded this Braintree lawyer's wife that English law gave a married woman little recourse against a brutal, selfish husband. His right to chastise her as he would a disobedient child, though circumscribed with provisions against violence, remained from the Middle Ages. He controlled her property, directed her labor, and provided her subsistence, for she stood in the same relationship to him as the indentured servant to his master. In any disagreement over these reciprocal rights and duties, the advantage obviously lay with the husband.

Massachusetts in practice had liberalized and humanized the English law, both in response to New World conditions and in the absence of the ecclesiastical courts that in the mother country had jurisdiction over marriages. Divorces, though still not numerous, were easier to obtain in Massachusetts; and an occasional woman retained her property rights by a prenuptial contract with the bridegroom-to-be. But the recent rise of a more professional and better-trained colonial bar, well versed in Blackstone—of which John Adams was a prime example—threatened to bring colonial law into greater harmony with the English. Abigail saw with remarkable clarity that colonial independence promised not only freedom from taxation by the British Parliament but also a

grand opportunity for Americans to preserve and
extend their improvements over the harsher features of English law.

She did not specify what legal reforms would
accomplish her purpose. She never advocated
that women vote, hold public office, or otherwise cross into the public orbit of the male. She
wanted a separate legal existence for the married
woman that would make it easier for a wife to
institute an action against an abusive husband,
that would guarantee her a share of the fruits of
their mutual labors, and that would recognize
her voice in the education of daughters. Abigail
Adams pleaded not for herself but for all those
women who, unlike her, had not found a Sir
Charles Grandison behind whose protective
shield their femininity could flourish.

Two weeks later John Adams laughingly answered his wife's ultimatum. He had heard that
the Revolution had "loosened the bands of Government every where" and planted seeds of unrest
among young people, Indians, and Negroes. But
Abigail's letter was "the first Intimation that another Tribe more numerous and powerfull than
all the rest were grown discontented." She could
be certain that men knew better than to repeal
their "Masculine systems": "Altho they are in full
Force, you know they are little more than Theory.
We dare not exert our Power in its full Latitude.

We are obliged to go fair, and softly, and in Practice you know We are the subjects. We have only the Name of Masters, and rather than give up this, which would compleatly subject Us to the Despotism of the Peticoat, I hope General Washington, and all our brave Heroes would fight."

John Adams facetiously raised the ancient myth of petticoat rule, knowing that the give-and-take existing in their marriage might lead some of their friends and neighbors to see Abigail as a domineering wife. By treating her "Code of Laws" as a joke, he saved her the embarrassment of seriously prosecuting a case against one of the least guilty of men. She suggested to Mercy Otis Warren the possibility of their joining in a petition to the Congress, but then dropped the subject with a final retort:

> I can not say that I think you very generous to the Ladies, for whilst you are proclaiming peace and good will to Men, Emancipating all Nations, you insist upon retaining an absolute power over Wives. But you must remember that Arbitrary power is like most other things which are very hard, very liable to be broken—and notwithstanding all your wise Laws and Maxims we have it in our power not only to free ourselves but to subdue our Masters, and without voilence throw both your natural and legal authority at our feet—
> "Charm by accepting, by submitting sway
> Yet have our Humour most when we obey."

To Mrs. Warren she confided, "I have only been making trial of the Disintresstedness of his Virtue, and when weigh'd in the balance have found it wanting." Which was to say that not even the kindest and most generous of men, not even John Adams, could be trusted with arbitrary power.

The husband's prolonged absences had begun to produce subtle changes in their relationship. In the spring of 1776 she busied herself with such domestic chores as making soap and home-spun clothes; and, like many other wives with absent husbands, she took over management of the farm. The war had brought a labor shortage and high wages; consequently she had difficulty securing farmhands and was forced to hire a "Negro fellow" to work under her direction and to pay highly for the labor of one of their ten-ants. She also faced decisions concerning the dis-posal of a barge of which John was part owner, the renting of their Boston house, the breeding of livestock, and an unexpected opportunity to purchase choice land. John heaped praise on the management of his "Farmeress," joking that "our Neighbours will think Affairs more dis-creetly conducted in my Absence than at any other Time." Warmed by his approval, she sometimes now referred to "*our* own private af-fairs" or "*our* House at Boston," whereas in the past it had always been "*your*" business or "*your*" property. John continued to speak of "*my* affairs at home," and she reverted to the deferential pronoun when pleading for him to return and lift such unwomanly responsibilities from her shoulders. Yet both sensed the large measure of managerial as well as psychological dependence he had come to place on her and the resulting reciprocity in their marriage.

John and Abigail Adams were groping their way toward an understanding of the role of women in the new republic. He was willing to admit that females were theoretically included in the governed whose consent gave moral legitimacy to a government. In general, however, he held that their delicacy, domesticity, and primary concern for their children left them much more valuable as a private influence on husbands and sons than they could possibly be in any public political capacity. Behind nearly every great man of history, he argued, there had been a woman of unusual knowledge and ambition. Abigail was prepared to accept this developing view that the enlightened wife and mother, working in the private world of the home, would be the main instrument for the inculcation of those virtues essential for the survival of a free republic. But how, she inquired in the month after independence, can the republic produce "Heroes, Statesmen and Philosophers" if it did not also produce "learned women"? And she could not hide her disappointment when the final copy of the Declaration of Independence omitted the strong statement against slavery contained in an early draft sent by John. He had not even replied to her concern for slaves as well as women. Instead he worked in the Congress to eliminate anything in the Declaration that would alienate the southern colonies. She was learning what the founders of the new nation meant when they wrote that "all men are created equal."

IV

"Bereft of My Better Half"

1776–1778

A more immediate threat to her family than British arms restrained Abigail's elation over the Declaration of Independence. The wartime movement of soldiers and civilians had stirred up a widespread epidemic of smallpox. Disease then occupied the center stage of the Revolution, pushing military operations into the wings. John Adams was not far wrong when he exclaimed to his wife in June 1776, "The Small Pox is ten times more terrible than Britons, Canadians and Indians together."

The mother could not hope to spare herself and the children, none of whom had developed immunity either naturally through recovery from the disease or artificially through inoculation. She feared even to inspect their house in Boston, the town with the most victims. Since persons being inoculated became themselves carriers of the plague, the Boston selectmen refused to permit inoculation until the full extent of the epidemic became clear at the beginning of July. Once they made their decision, the town turned into one large isolation hospital in which eventually nearly five thousand persons, many from outlying towns, underwent inoculation.

Knowing that her husband had already given his approval, Abigail did not hesitate. She, her four children, the Cranch family, sister Betsy, Uncle Cotton Tufts, and one of John's law clerks moved into Uncle Isaac Smith's Boston mansion to join those being inoculated. Their quarters were comfortable, and they had driven a cow from Braintree to supply milk. John Hancock in Philadelphia hastened to offer his mansion—the best in Boston—with all its staff and facilities. It pleased Abigail that she was already well situated, for the last thing she wanted was to be indebted to Hancock, who she thought had begun to take on princely airs.

Inoculation (or variolation), practiced in Boston since the 1720s, was a simple if dangerous medical procedure. The physician made a small slit in the arm, inserted a drop of pus taken from an infected person, and closed the incision with a bandage. Then followed an uneasy wait for results, which ranged from death or disfigurement to the complete absence of signs of success. The statistical knowledge that the chances of survival through inoculation were at least ten times better than if one contracted smallpox naturally never entirely eased the mind of a person being deliberately infected with the great killer disease of the age.

On July 11 and 12, Dr. Bulfinch inoculated Mrs. Adams, Nabby, and the boys. The mother grieved to see her children—the oldest eleven and the youngest not yet four—subjected to such a risk, but she understood her duty. While waiting hopefully for symptoms to develop, she ventured out on the eighteenth to attend a church service of thanksgiving for independence. She heard the Declaration read from the State House balcony and saw the king's arms and other symbols of royal authority taken down and burned. "Thus ends royall Authority in this State," she wrote to Philadelphia, "and all the people shall say Amen."

At Uncle Smith's the painful suspense continued. Smallpox began with a high fever, severe headache, pains in the lower body, and vomiting. A few days after the onset, the patient broke out in red spots that soon erupted into pus-filled pimples. If inoculation failed to bring on these telltale signs in ten days to two weeks, the physicians might repeat the process. The symptoms of the mother and eldest son developed on schedule with just sufficient pocks to indicate success (Abigail had only three). Nabby was so slightly ill that it was thought best to reinoculate, and Tommy had three injections of pus before the symptoms appeared. After three unsuccessful inoculations, Charles contracted a serious case believed to be "in the natural way." His recovery was in doubt as he lay delirious for two days with an "exceeding high fever and most plentifull Eruption." Nabby also suffered the worst horror of smallpox. From her second inoculation, according to her mother, she developed more than a thousand eruptions as large as a "great Green Pea" and could neither stand nor sit for days.

By the end of August the worst was over, and early in September the family was back home. But even the return trip had been a reminder of the deadly plague. Their belongings had been thoroughly smoked as they crossed the quarantine line established at the entry to Boston, and they underwent further purification at the Cranches' before entering their own house. Charles remained weak and in isolation for some time. He had endured his illness with such patience and humor that he was

now generally acknowledged to be the most engaging of the Adams children. Nabby resigned
herself to accepting the gratuitous advice of her el-
ders on how to restore her complexion or, failing
that, to compensate with inner beauty. From
Philadelphia the father advised his "little Speck-
eled Beauty" to avoid the sun as the best means of
keeping her pits from "being lasting and conspicuous." Abigail felt only gratitude and relief. When
preparing to leave Boston, she wrote John, "I
came here with all my treasure of children, have
passd thro one of the most terrible Diseases to
which humane Nature is subject, and not one of us
is wanting." John knew and summarized what this
month and a half ordeal had meant for Abigail
Adams: "It is an important Event in a Mans Life,
to go thro that distemper. It is a very great Thing,
for a whole Family, to get well over it."

During her confinement Mrs. Adams had to
brace herself against a rumor that her husband
had been poisoned in New York while on his way
home. She believed the loyalists capable of such a
deed but bravely discounted the report. Once back
in Braintree her spirits were temporarily lifted by
the family's return to health and a round of company. Then, after a summer of high expense and
neglect of the farm, she came face to face with the
reality of wartime inflation. She appealed to John
to come home before all his property was lost and

his family was "wanting Bread." By this time she had abandoned hope that Massachusetts would ever adequately compensate its delegates to Congress. John, homesick himself, yielded to her plea and set out from Philadelphia on October 13. After a separation of ten months, the ecstasy of their reunion knew no limit.

Since the birth of Tommy in 1772, Abigail had avoided conception. Now quickly after John's return she became pregnant. Possibly she secretly, even unconsciously, wanted a baby as a way of keeping John home. More likely, they had discussed the question and agreed that he would not return to Congress in the event she became pregnant. Or conception may have been entirely accidental, as so often happened in an age when birth control depended largely on willpower. Just thirty-two, she was not beyond the normal childbearing age, and with a husband at her side might have welcomed an addition to the family, especially a second daughter.

Before they knew of Abigail's pregnancy, John was elected to serve another year in Congress. They had only nine weeks together, including a pleasant one in Boston, until he rode away again on January 9. By then both were certain of her condition. "No seperation was ever so painfull to me," she wrote after him. To Mercy Otis Warren she dressed her grief with patriotism: "I had it in my Heart to disswade him from going and I know I could have prevaild, but our publick affairs at the time wore so gloomy an aspect that I thought if ever his assistance was wanted, it must be at such a time." No wife ever understood a husband better. She knew that if he remained at her insistence the unanswered call of duty would deeply scar his soul.

John attempted to atone for his guilt by writing more often and more tenderly than he had in the past. He wrote four letters to her one, a frequency she noticed with joy. But not until May, with warmer weather and the renewal of social life, did she overcome her depression. Until then she had "many melancholy Hours" while thinking of her situation and the danger John faced now that the war had moved southward. With the exception of painful eyes—a disorder she blamed on inoculation—her health was better than during past pregnancies. Still her mind sometimes turned to the ever present possibility of death in childbirth, a fear increased when a friend, the wife of a prominent Boston minister, died in April of a postpartum infection. She poured out her apprehension to John: "How great the mind that can overcome the fear of Death! How anxious the Heart of a parent who looks round upon a family of young and helpless children and thinks of leaving them to a

World full of snares and temptations which they have neither discretion to foresee, nor prudence to avoid."

By June Abigail looked forward to her delivery with growing anxiety: "I wish the day passt, yet dread its arrival." John joked that she might have twins, a bit of humor she was in no mood to appreciate. During the first week of July she took ill with symptoms she had not experienced in previous pregnancies. A twentieth-century obstetrician would have suspected toxemia and have taken preventive measures. But neither the midwife nor the physician of Abigail's day could diagnose or treat that complication. On the night of July 8 she was taken with a "shaking fit," apparently the convulsions associated with serious toxemia. Despite the assurances of Dr. Tufts and her sisters, she no longer felt life within her. Labor began on the evening of the tenth, at about the time a letter from John was handed her. She answered the letter between contractions, writing not only of her condition but of the high prices of food, the problems of the farm, and the course of the war. After a quiet night, she gave birth the next day—John Quincy's tenth birthday—to a "very fine Babe," a girl with her eyes shut in death "as tho they were only closed for sleep."

Nabby cried for hours over the sister she had lost, but the premonition of the baby's death spared Abigail much of the initial shock and grief. She gave thanks that her life had been saved and for an unusually short postnatal confinement. The mails continued to bring letters from John expressing his hope for a "little female Beauty." But perhaps the most difficult moment came the next month when she first went out to church again. On that Sunday she watched the baptism of a niece named for John's mother. Now she felt her bereavement "with all its poignancy," for the stillborn baby was to have received the name of Abigail's "own dear Mother." Throughout these weeks she analyzed her emotions closely in letters to John. She did not feel for this unknown daughter what she had felt for little Susanna, whose babyish wiles she had enjoyed for a year. Rather, this loss drew her closer to husband and family. Even the sight of a piece of John's clothing brought a thrill as a reminder of their love, while also giving pain at the thought of the distance separating them. Most of all, she resolved to devote herself more than ever to the welfare of their living children. After losing two daughters, she grieved that Nabby would never have a sister. In most middle-class homes, mothers concentrated on raising daughters and fathers on sons. The natural mother-daughter tie between Abigail and Nabby now drew closer that ever; yet, with John away, this mother felt an

equal obligation to turn her sons into worthy citizens of the new nation. This childbirth experience had profound effects on the mother and on
her family.

Throughout her pregnancy Abigail had con-
tended with the shortage of foodstuffs in east-
ern Massachusetts. In Boston some people went
hungry, and merchants withheld what supplies
they had in an effort to defeat the government's
plan to regulate prices. Outlying districts like
Braintree were somewhat better off, and John
eased his family's situation in March 1777 by
sending a barrel of flour on one of Uncle
Smith's ships. Yet in April Abigail simply refused to buy fresh meat at the prevailing price
and fed the family what was left of the salt
meat from last fall. With veiled delight she recounted the incident in July when a mob of
Boston females forced an "eminent, wealthy,
stingy" merchant to surrender the keys to his
warehouse, from which they confiscated a
hogshead of coffee held for a higher price. She
wrote John that money had depreciated by
three-quarters and that barter was replacing
cash transactions. By diligent management she
paid their taxes, collected some of the debts
owed John, and had enough left to send a sum
to the Continental Loan Office—the equivalent
of buying a war bond. As for clothes, she pur-

chased no more than had "Adam and Eve in innocence." She and the children dressed in neither "fine linnen nor scarlet," she proudly informed John, but in the "plain and decent manufactory" of the family.

In August Abigail's Negro farmhand deserted her in the middle of the haying season to claim a bounty for enlisting in the army. Somehow she managed to get in abundant crops of hay, flax, corn, and vegetables. She had sufficient beef, pork, butter, and cheese, but had to live without sugar, molasses, tea, and coffee, imports no longer available except at black market prices. Though John praised her husbandry, she protested that she merely struggled to prevent their falling into ruin. Actually, during this year of separation Abigail developed a degree of confidence in her judgment that could no longer be hidden by language deferential to the male. Among other examples, she tactfully settled a dispute over the renting of their Boston house and rejected John's advice to sell a horse he had sent home from Philadelphia.

Abigail displayed another side of her independence when sister Betsy accepted John Shaw's proposal of marriage. Teaching school at Weymouth while waiting for a pulpit to open, Shaw had lived at the Smith parsonage. Abigail took a dislike to him from the beginning and warned

Betsy against any involvement, an admonition that brought forth an eloquent and forceful expression of resentment. By the time Shaw was ordained minister of the Haverhill church early in 1777, John knew that a wedding was planned and requested his wife to pay his respects to the couple. She flatly refused. It was a subject she could not bring herself even to mention to Betsy, who in Abigail's view had been driven to marrying beneath her by the fear of turning into a spinster at twenty-seven.

Abigail regarded Shaw as a man of no taste. Furthermore, he was a Calvinist with a tendency to be dogmatic. Perhaps also she unconsciously regretted the youngest sister's abandoning their aging father by moving a considerable distance north of Boston. After the wedding in October, she merely wrote John that among several recent marriages was that of Miss Smith to Mr. Shaw. When Betsy's first baby arrived the following year, Abigail almost sneered: "I have a new Nephew at Haverhill (betterd I hope by the Mothers side)." For her part, Betsy remained undaunted and repeatedly showed her brilliance and good nature in preserving a warm relationship with a sister who at first detested her husband. But she also declared her independence by signing her letters "Elizabeth," and no longer "Betsy." Girls usually kept their nicknames for life (as Nabby did) while boys gave them up as adult men. Mrs. Shaw was now the mistress of a handsome parsonage in the thriving trading town of Haverhill, near the New Hampshire border, where social life far outdid anything she had experienced in Weymouth. Her duties were increased by the burden of caring for the boys Shaw prepared for Harvard, eventually including the Adams sons. Elizabeth had a mind of her own. For example, she disagreed strongly with Abigail's insistence on being bled for most ailments. And she had a baby at the age of forty despite her sister's advice that she was too old.

The long separations of Abigail and John significantly changed their lives and those of their children. Being what she called a "widow" for half her married life made Mrs. Adams much more independent than the typical middle-class wife. As one result, she became freer in associations with the men outside the family with whom she conducted business; and during the remainder of her life she had a number of significant intellectual friendships with other men, usually younger ones. For the present, after the crisis of her last pregnancy, a growing self-confidence permitted a more romantic view of the absent husband. In contrast to past restraint, she referred to John as "my Love," and trusted to the uncertain mails other endearing expressions such as "wholly

Yours" and "words cannot convey to you the tenderness of my affection." One letter in September 1777 closed with "Good Night Friend of my Heart, companion of my youth—Husband and Lover—Angels watch thy Repose." She was discovering the truth few women of her century were privileged to learn, that even a limited equality in a marriage freed the love of a wife for her husband from the inhibitions of masculine domination. In another way too, it was easier to love a husband hundreds of miles distant: epistolary affection posed no threat of pregnancy. This passionate couple may have silently regarded separation as an incentive to abstinence.

As another consequence of their separations, Abigail romanticized the absent father to his children. Little Tommy, just five, hardly knew John Adams and must have regarded him as some godlike creature who came home for short rests between creating new worlds. The older children, as they read their father's letters of advice and instruction and listened to their mother recount his contributions to the struggle for independence, escaped or at least postponed that sad awakening of a child to the imperfections of a parent. To his sons especially, John Adams by 1777 had become more of a symbol of what they should aspire to be than a parent. Their mother understood what was happening, though she knew not how to prevent it. She believed one of the greatest sacrifices they made for their country was the separation of the father from his children "at a time of life when the joint instructions and admonition of parents sink deeper than in maturer years."

For Abigail the year following the Declaration of Independence had never been so filled with personal problems as to drive the war from her thoughts. There had been little good news since the evacuation of Boston. The British army returned to strike at New York in late summer 1776. After an unsuccessful peace conference on Staten Island, in which John Adams participated, Washington's army narrowly escaped total defeat near New York City. In the Christmas season two American victories in the middle colonies cheered the hearts of patriots; but Washington could not stop the British from occupying Philadelphia in the fall of 1777 and forcing members of Congress to flee from their beds. That same summer General John Burgoyne marched south from Canada to cut the colonies in two. Then at last American prayers were answered. After some little successes, Burgoyne found himself surrounded in the fall by superior forces in upper New York and accepted the generous surrender terms offered him.

When the news of this glorious victory reached Braintree the last week in October, Abigail took Nabby and rode to Boston to join with her friends at the Brattle Street Church in a service of "thanksgiving and praise to the Supreem Being who hath so remarkably deliverd our Enimies into our Hands." She heard the eloquent Dr. Cooper compare the American states, particularly the New England ones, to the ancient Israelites who had been led by God from a land of "civil and religious Tyranny" to a country where they enjoyed freedom. One passage of the sermon held an ominous note for the future of the Adamses. This leading Congregational preacher, who in the past from his pulpit had associated French Catholics with the forces of hell, now pronounced his holy blessing on the king of France and gratefully acknowledged that monarch's support of the colonies with military supplies.

Her sacrifices had only hardened Abigail's attitude toward the mother country and freed her mind of the slightest doubt that her countrymen would fight until independence was won. In her view, religious infidelity had so weakened the British character that Englishmen had thrown off "all regard to their fellow creatures and to those precepts and doctrines which require peace and good will to Men." She took advantage of Burgoyne's surrender to deliver an epistolary lecture to her cousin, Reverend Isaac Smith, Jr., who had disappointed his family by letting loyalist sympathies induce him to accept a pastorate in England during the war. After reviewing the suffering of the colonies, she announced to this Tory cousin that Americans would never again be the "Slaves of Britains" and "that the invincible american Spirit is as far from being conquerd as it was the day the cruel mandates [the Coercive Acts of 1774] were issued against her. She gathers strength by oppression and grows firmer by resistance. Tis the cause of truth and justice and will finally prevail tho the combined force of Earth and hell rise against it."

While the members of Congress scrambled by a circuitous route from Philadelphia to the security of York, Pennsylvania, Mrs. Adams went three anxious weeks without news of her husband's whereabouts. Her fears had scarcely been relieved by a letter when another announced that he was coming home. After only six weeks at York, he and Samuel Adams set off for Massachusetts in the middle of November 1777. John had earlier promised, "The next Time I come home, shall be for a long Time." At their joyous reunion on November 27, Abigail sensed that he meant to keep his promise and take up the practice of law once more. There was an all-too-short rest in Braintree before the middle of December found him in Portsmouth, New Hampshire, trying a maritime case. She understood why he had gone again so soon: now that he had come home to stay, he had to recoup some of the financial losses they had suffered while he had served his country. But except for court dates, his family could expect him home from now on. The "widowhood" of Mrs. Adams had ended, or so she thought.

Her anticipation of domestic bliss soon vanished. While John was still in New Hampshire, a letter from Congress reached Braintree notifying him of his appointment as one of the three commissioners representing the United States in France. Opening the letter without waiting for her husband, Abigail at first raged against this plot to rob her of all happiness. With John gone, she gathered her thoughts in a letter to James Lovell, the Massachusetts congressman who had sent the notification of appointment, and once more the epistolary style shaped her thinking. By the time she had finished she had moved the issue from her emotions to the higher ground of public duty. "At the expence both of food and sleep," she had brought herself to face this new crisis with "fortitude and resignation." Not too upset to appreciate the honor done John by his country, she now determined to stand back and leave the decision to him. Consequently, she sent the letter from Congress to Boston so that he would receive it sooner on the return journey. In her calm moments she had little doubt of his answer. From almost the beginning of their life together she had learned that John Adams knew not how to turn his back on public responsibility. He rushed home and within a few hours wrote a letter of acceptance. Aside from a faint lament at the continued loss of income, the only real hesitation was over his lack of the language. But the scholar in him suppressed that doubt by resolving to master as much French as possible on the long voyage to Europe.

Much more troublesome was the question of whether to take the family with him. Abigail wanted to go and at first insisted on it. But in the next few weeks the realities of ocean travel in wartime gradually overcame their desire to avoid another long separation. In addition to the normal hazards of a winter crossing, the British navy preyed daily on American shipping. John could not bear the possibility of his wife and some of the children being destitute in England while he rotted in the Tower of London as a prisoner of war. He thought it safest to go alone but finally gave in to the pleas of John Quincy to accompany him. Abigail would remain home with Nabby and the two younger boys.

Consenting to the departure of her eldest son intensified Abigail's agony at the prospect of a new widowhood. Six months before his eleventh birthday, Johnny (as the family called him) had not yet demonstrated the precocity that would mark his mid-teens. But his lively conversation had helped warm his mother's lonely hours. Though she treated him more and more like an adult, he remained a boy who liked outdoor recreation as much as study and who resisted all efforts to dress him neatly. In his mother's mind he had reached the most impressionable age. Could he, she wondered, withstand the "many snares and temptations" of Europe "which may stain his morals even at this early period of life"? Nevertheless, she knew that "to exclude him from temptation would be to exclude him from the World in which he is to live." Worried whether her maternal teaching and example had been sufficient to "padlock" his mind against evil, she also recognized the advantages of a stay in Europe under the watchful eye of his father.

Fearful of British spies, John told only a few essential persons of his appointment and embarked from Braintree rather than Boston. Abigail numbed her pain by keeping busy getting her departing loved ones ready for their voyage. The sad farewell came on February 13, 1778. All the children shed tears except Johnny, who struggled to preserve a "manly firmness." With "full Heart and weeping Eye," Abigail watched until her husband and son rode out of sight. A day later she unburdened herself in a letter to a young friend: "And now cannot you immagine me seated by my fire side Bereft of my better Half, and added to that a Limb lopt of to heighten the anguish. In vain have I summoned philosiphy, its aid is vain. Come then Religion thy force can alone support the Mind under the severest trials and hardest conflicts humane Nature is subject to."

For the next four months Abigail had little except religion to console her. She heard nothing but rumors that the ship had been lost or captured and that Franklin had been assassinated, a fate that might await the other commissioners. Not until mid-June did she learn from an English newspaper that her husband and son had arrived in France. Relieved that the two were safe for the moment, she turned her attention to the problems of surviving another period of separation. This time she could not even guess how long it might be.

V

"Patriotism in the Female Sex"

1778–1784

Abigail Adams was thirty-three in 1778. Years of ravenous reading and tireless letter writing had provided an education equalled by few women of the age. With the agony of the recent stillbirth fresh in her memory, she resolved to have no more pregnancies. Now that childbearing and inoculation were behind her, she had passed two major barriers to long life for females. A rational religious faith imbibed in youth had proved emotionally satisfying in adulthood. Her four surviving children were sacred charges to be reared in that faith and taught its major corollary, a true patriot's love of liberty. She had achieved a sufficient measure of intellectual independence from her husband to make possible a genuine affection for him as a whole person, rather than merely a dutiful loyalty to the man with whom she was bound until death. These elements of her life now fused in a maturity equal to accepting the turn of events that once again separated her from the "dearest of Friends and tenderest of Husbands."

Three thousand miles of ocean lay between Abigail and John for the next six and one-half years, save for a single period of four months. She daily lamented and often deplored their separation, but she never despaired. Instead, loneliness strengthened the conviction that John Adams performed a heroic task for his country and for the preservation of human freedom. Identifying with him and his work, she defended him against both real and imagined detractors. Simultaneously she placed a high value on the personal sacrifice she had made for the American cause by giving up for more than half their married life the companionship and support of a loving and potentially affluent husband. Such self-esteem overcame any doubts concerning the value of her position in the new political order of republican America.

France had entered into a formal alliance with the United States a few days before John Adams sailed for Europe. When his wife learned the good news, she experienced no difficulty in accepting the hated Catholic monarchy of her early years as the present defender of political and religious freedom. "Americans are now bound to transfer their affections" to France, she wrote, and "to eradicate all those national prejudices . . . craftily instilld" by their former connection with England.

Abigail felt a new sense of security when a French fleet—the first fruits of the alliance—appeared off the coast in August 1778. In the fall the comte d'Estaing anchored his storm-damaged ships in Boston Harbor for two months of refitting. He came ashore at Mount Wollaston on purpose to extend an invitation to the wife of Commissioner Adams to dine on his flagship with her family and friends. On the appointed day the admiral's barge took her party to the ship, where the reception exceeded all expectation. Before sailing from Boston, d'Estaing gave another dinner for Mrs. Adams—an "entertainment fit for a princess." In turn, she received visits in the humble Braintree cottage from several groups of officers, some of whom had the opportunity to sample her cooking. Pleasantly surprised at the decorum of the allied officers, she wrote John that "it would gratify me much if I had it in my power to entertain every officer in the Fleet." She regretted that as a girl she had learned to read French without speaking it.

With the treaties signed, John Adams found no major diplomatic challenge in France, only the endless routine business of the commission, much neglected by Franklin. But John had landed in the middle of controversy. The commissioner he had replaced, Silas Deane, returned home to a Congress divided over his conduct. His fellow commissioner, Arthur Lee, had loudly charged that Deane had profited in France by mixing public with private business. Deane retaliated in a newspaper address to the nation. By then both Franklin and the French foreign minister considered Lee an enemy to the alliance. John Adams, despite his suspicions of Deane, attempted to remain publicly impartial as long as possible.

Before she had heard from John on the subject, Abigail read Deane's address and grasped the potential for national harm in this strife. She appealed to a member of Congress to exert himself in countering the poison uncorked by Deane's diatribe. Her neighbors, she feared, would now believe any wild tale of corruption in Congress or its foreign service. Only after thus forcefully expressing herself did she ask pardon for taking up a subject regarded as "foreign to my sex." In the absence of a husband and in view of the "critical state" of the country, she had thought herself obligated to warn this delegate of the impending danger. It was regrettable, she exclaimed to Mercy Otis Warren, that "unworthy characters" like Deane "should stain our Anals and Lessen us in the Eyes of foreign powers." But such would always be the case where self-interest was "more powerfull than publick virtue."

Abigail learned little of John's mission abroad. Some letters went down with their ships or were thrown overboard to avoid interception by the royal navy. Then at times John let weeks slip by without writing at all. He hesitated to trust confidential news to those letters he did write; consequently, many were short. His wife's sharp though loving complaints drove him to reply, "For Gods sake never reproach me again with not writing. . . . Your Wounds are too deep. You know not—you feel not—the dangers that surround me, nor those that may be brought upon our Country."

But Mrs. Adams did not lack for other correspondents. A steady stream of mail kept her well informed. John Thaxter, Jr., her young cousin who had taken a secretarial position with Congress, wrote Abigail often, sending her all but the confidential transactions of that body. John had requested Thaxter to correspond with his wife, and he may have made the same request of James Lovell, a Massachusetts delegate to Congress. As secretary of the Committee of Foreign

Affairs, Lovell communicated with the diplomats abroad. But his long correspondence with
the wife of Commissioner Adams went beyond
official business.

A few years older than Abigail, Lovell had
grown up in Boston, where his father taught
school. Despite the stigma of fathering a bastard
child, he received his Harvard degree, married,
and settled down to the impecunious life of a
schoolmaster. He became such an ardent patriot
and Whig propagandist that when the war began
the British imprisoned him on the pretext of spying. Finally exchanged, he returned to Massachusetts a minor hero and was elected to Congress.
The Adamses had known Lovell well during their
days in Boston, where they attended the same
church. Abigail virtually demanded that, since
Congress had deprived her of a husband, Lovell
must communicate news of congressional activities to her. He willingly obliged. Without other
income or position, he remained in Congress for
five years, never once returning to his family. No
other congressman shouldered such a heavy burden of duties. He wrote Abigail regularly, sent
her the congressional journals, and rendered a
variety of services. She saw in this man who had
survived a cruel imprisonment "with unshaken
fortitude" a source of "that hidden strength" she
needed to endure her own ordeal.

By the time John Adams stepped ashore in France, Lovell's letters were becoming teasingly flirtatious. He professed a "*secret* Admiration" for this "lovely Woman," and admitted his envy of her husband. She labeled him a "very dangerous Man" in a long letter that did little to discourage this correspondent whom she also called a "most ingenious and agreable flatterer." Many of Lovell's letters were businesslike, but when lonesome or bored he resumed his expressions of affection. She refused to believe the rumors of his immorality and excused her freedom in writing to him out of a love for everyone attached to her absent husband. Their correspondence was not clandestine. She wrote John of her "attentive Friend," and he informed her husband of his letters to the "lovely Portia," Abigail's pen name.

It was all harmless—one lonely person to another—or, as he closed one of his letters, "Very platonically to be sure but, very, very affectionately." Abigail was flattered by his attention and recognized how much pleasure he received from this literary dalliance. When he teased her with sexual suggestiveness in the humorous fashion of the novelist Laurence Sterne, she scolded him for being a "wicked Man." Yes, she admitted, she had read and admired the purest of Sterne's works, but absolutely refused to open his most risqué novel, *Tristram Shandy,* of which Lovell was fond. She advised him to return to his wife and relieve the tensions of associating exclusively with his male colleagues in Congress. Cooled a bit by this response from a "lovely Moralist," he became more restrained for awhile. Nonetheless, their intimate correspondence continued during Lovell's long stint in Congress, with Abigail sometimes complaining when he did not promptly answer her letters. As a genuine epistolary friendship slowly developed between the two, Abigail supressed her fear that the British would intercept and publish one of Lovell's most suggestive letters. This lonesome congressman would not be the last man smitten by the wife of John Adams.

Usually solemn if not melancholy, John occasionally teased his wife. Soon after reaching France, he wrote that he envied Dr. Franklin's freedom with the ladies of Paris, who permitted the venerable philosopher to embrace and kiss them as often as he pleased. Abigail suggested in reply that a "grave American republican" like Commissioner Adams ought to be shocked at such practices, and she turned this playful exchange into one of her typical laments over the defects of female education in America. The accomplishments of many French ladies, she had read, resulted from their being permitted to develop their distinctive feminine talents to the fullest.

What a regrettable contrast to the "trifling narrow contracted Education" of females in this country! "You need not be told," she reminded him once again, "how much female Education is neglected, nor how fashonable it has been to ridicule Female learning."

In the fall of 1778 Congress dissolved the commission and made Franklin its sole minister to the French court. Adams had recommended such a measure and was pleased to be extracted from the Deane controversy. When Congress neither recalled nor reassigned him, he resolved to return home. He and his son sailed from France in June 1779 and reached Braintree at the beginning of August, delighted to be reunited with the family yet appreciative of their exposure to French culture.

After a short rest, Adams plunged into the work of the Massachusetts Constitutional Convention. More than anyone else he shaped this frame of government, ratified in 1780, that became the model for the federal constitution of 1787. It is uncertain whether his wife learned of his opposition to female suffrage in debates over the new constitution. As he labored over the political structure of republican Massachusetts, early in October word arrived from Philadelphia that Congress had unanimously chosen Adams the sole minister plenipotentiary to negotiate peace with Great Britain. He never hesitated. Both the unanimity of the election and the challenge of bringing the war to a successful conclusion rendered this mission irresistible.

Then followed a series of anguished decisions. John still did not want to subject his wife and daughter to the rigors of the Atlantic in winter. "A Lady cannot help being an odious creature at sea," he told Abigail. But sons were different. Though Johnny had no desire for another voyage, his mother insisted. He now knew the French language and was thus ready to benefit more fully from European travel. This woman had read of the heroes of Greece and Rome, had absorbed the libertarian maxims of the seventeenth-century English Whigs, and had watched her countrymen defend their liberties in battle. She thus felt qualified to tell her son that "these are times in which a Genious would wish to live." Did the twelve-year-old Johnny not know that the "Character of the Hero and the Statesman" is formed by facing the challenges of a great period of history? And not the least of his motivations should be pride in having "a parent who has taken so large and active a share in this contest, and discharged the trust reposed in him with so much satisfaction as to be honourd with the important Embassy, which at present calls him abroad." Johnny could not resist such a mother. She later observed with satisfaction that he "readily submitted" to her advice.

Abigail also urged that Charles accompany his father and brother. Though delicate in health, at nine he was ready for the serious schooling that would prepare him for Harvard. She did not feel equal to the task of arranging tutors for the older boys. Besides, she believed they had reached an age when a father's care was more necessary than a mother's.

On November 13, 1779, Abigail and John parted again. Seeing the lovable Charles leave multiplied her grief. His tears, "shed at parting," she wrote a year later, "have melted my Heart a thousand times." As John waited on board for a favorable wind, she sent a pathetic note after him: "My habitation, how disconsolate it looks! My table I set down to it but cannot swallow my food. O Why was I born with so much Sensibility and why possessing it have I so often been call'd to struggle with it?"

Abigail remained in Braintree with a household of Nabby, Tommy, a niece, and two servants. For weeks they were nearly shut in by one of the worst winters in New England history. Boston Harbor, never before completely frozen, was so solid in February that Nabby took a shortcut across the ice to pay her annual winter visit to Uncle Isaac Smith. But at least Abigail no longer had the care of the farm, which had been let to tenants. Still the family finances and other property remained entirely in her hands. John had arranged for two Boston merchants—in addition to Uncle Smith—to advise her on money matters, and the always faithful Dr. Cotton Tufts was nearby in Weymouth. The decisions were hers, however.

In spite of a depreciating currency, inflated prices, and ever increasing taxes, Abigail preserved her husband's estate while he was dependent on the uncertain and dilatory actions of Congress for his salary and expenses. She received rental income from the farm and the Boston house, and she never gave up trying to collect the legal fees still owed John. In addition they had some money in public securities, though the interest was difficult to collect. When she ran short of cash she drew on her husband in France with a bill of exchange—the eighteenth-century merchant's substitute for a check—which would eventually make its way through mercantile channels and, duly discounted, finally reach the banker who handled the large sums France loaned the United States. It was a risky transaction because Congress sometimes spent money faster than its diplomats could borrow it from friendly European nations.

A little experience taught Abigail that European goods were her best hedge against inflation.

Scarce luxury items could coax out of tight pockets whatever little sums of hard money people had saved. She requested John to send not only supplies for the family but a small but regular shipment of "saleable articles" to be sold for her by a son of Dr. Tufts who had gone into trade. And so they arrived: a large variety of cloth and dress trimmings, handkerchiefs of all sorts, gloves, fans, pins, bedticking, dishes, silverware, tea, and more. Profits from these sales enabled her to satisfy the tax collector. At the same time, mother and daughter appeared better dressed than in the early years of the war when they had boasted of wearing homespun.

John implicitly trusted Abigail's management, even on the question of purchasing land adjoining their farm. Only once did he seriously question her judgment. When in 1782 she made a speculative investment in Vermont lands, he gave her a direct order: "Dont meddle any more with Vermont." Undaunted, she stood her ground and offered to back this investment with land inherited from her father. There the matter rested, though in time, as John had predicted, the speculative bubble burst and the Vermont lands declined in value.

In detailing her management to John, Abigail now habitually used such expressions as "my own affairs." Finally, in a long letter concerning their funds and property, she awakened to the implication of her pronouns and apologized: "Forgive me if I sometimes use the singular instead of the plural, alass I have been too much necessitated to it." She forgot that when they were first separated in 1774 she had written not of *my* affairs or *ours* but of *yours*.

Abigail heard from John less than ever after his return to France. In the first months of 1780 she received several letters describing his safe arrival in Spain, where the captain made port with his leaky vessel. Then, after John had led his party on a rigorous winter journey over the Pyrenees into France, his letters reached Braintree with decreasing frequency. She went the first eight months of 1781 without a single line from him. Unwilling to sit idly until peace negotiations began, he had moved to Holland to seek a loan to bolster the collapsing congressional financial structure. The boys attended Dutch schools until in July 1781 Johnny set out on an even greater adventure. He traveled to Saint Petersburg as secretary and companion to the family's close friend Francis Dana, the first minister of the United States to Russia. By this time Charles was ill and so homesick that he insisted on returning to Massachusetts. His father agreed and arranged for a passage.

Abigail knew nothing of these developments for months. From other sources she first learned news of the boys. She was particularly unhappy that John, wanting to spare her worry, had not explained why Charles was sailing home. Her anxiety increased when he did not arrive as scheduled. For two months she believed he had gone down at sea. Then he reached Braintree late in January 1782 to describe how his journey had been delayed by an unexpected stay in Spain.

Now approaching his twelfth birthday, Charles had exercised his unique "faculty of gaining Hearts" across Europe. On the trek through Spain, John Thaxter had written Abigail, "The Charms of My little Friend Charley attract the Attention of every Body." The father himself, no sentimentalist, admitted that Charles was "a delightful little fellow" whom he loved "too much." The Parisians adored this blond lad, and so did the Dutch. From Amsterdam John wrote that wherever Charles goes "he gets the Hearts of every Body especially the Ladies."

When the delicate health of this pleasing lad had suffered from the damp climate of Holland, the father wearied of having a homesick child on his hands. By the time Charles reached home, he had regained his health. His mother found him taller and his agreeable manners more polished. She noticed in how many ways he took after his father, so much so that some called him a miniature John Adams. Abigail worried less than she had earlier that he would "be spoilt by being a favorite." She sent him and Tommy to live with her sister at Haverhill and to be tutored by their Uncle Shaw, whose merit she was at last beginning to acknowledge.

Abigail could scarcely conceive of her eldest son observing his fifteenth birthday nearly two thousand miles northeast of France in the Russian empire. Yet she rose to the occasion by charging him to observe carefully everything of value in that country and to commit his observations to writing. Especially must he compare Russia's monarchy with the American republican governments and note the "advantages and disadvantages arising from each." She cautioned him again to do nothing that would reflect upon his father's high station.

After fourteen months at the Russian court, John Quincy left Saint Petersburg in the fall of 1782, alone except for an Italian count traveling the same route. He spent the winter in Sweden and Denmark and in the spring reached his father's residence at The Hague. Abigail had received only one letter from Russia, and her husband had forwarded little news of their son. At last in November 1783 arrived a long letter detailing his return trip, and shortly afterwards came another full of observations on Russia. Although "the government of Russia is entirely despotical," Johnny reported, he had witnessed the common man's irrepressible craving for liberty. At sixteen, John Quincy Adams had mastered his mother's teaching concerning the principles of human freedom.

At home Abigail saw new threats to hard-won American liberties. She took great pride in her husband's contribution to the Massachusetts Constitution. Yet even that splendid frame of government would suffer if the voters elected an unfit man to the governor's office. When the first election approached in the fall of 1780, she knew that John Hancock would be the popular choice, though in her eyes he was a "tinkleling cymball," the practitioner of all the "low mean Arts" that could draw unthinking people to him. She favored James Bowdoin, the candidate of "merrit and integrity," who would have "the votes of the sensible judicious part of the State." Not even a woman of Abigail's education and administrative responsibility could vote, but she tried to exert influence in her private sphere. "If I cannot be a voter upon this occasion," she declared, "I will be a writer of votes." She campaigned in her town for Bowdoin, though well aware that Hancock's popularity could not be overcome.

As she watched Hancock returned to office each year with only slight opposition, Abigail saw him as the "golden Calf" before whom abler men were sacrificed; and she developed a distrust of democratic politics that intensified throughout her life. Like her friends the Warrens, she was incensed when in one of the darkest moments of the war "his Excellency gave a very Grand Ball, to introduce our Republican form of Government properly upon the Stage." And she joined the chorus of those who ridiculed Hancock's gout as a psychosomatic ailment that conveniently took him to his bed whenever he faced a difficult or unpopular decision. She readily accepted the flattering comment of friends who confided in her that when John Adams returned to his home state, the voters would at once acknowledge him to be the "disinterested patriot" who could direct the Commonwealth of Massachusetts back to the path of republican virtue. After the election of 1783 she informed John that some of Hancock's votes came from those who thought it unwise to elect a worthier governor only to turn him out in one year when a greater man returned from his diplomatic duties in Europe.

Hancock could be tolerated temporarily as an object lesson in the need for public virtue. Not so Franklin. John's letters from France had destroyed Abigail's reverence for the Sage of Philadelphia. By 1781 she classified Franklin with Deane and Benedict Arnold as Americans who had disgraced their country. Since the preceding summer John Adams had been at odds with Vergennes, the French foreign minister, who had preferred Franklin as the peace negotiator and who now insisted that all negotiations follow the lead of the French court. When Adams persisted in pursuing an independent course, Vergennes appealed to his friend Franklin for support. In a letter to Congress, Franklin intimated that Adams's independence threatened the alliance. His comments played into the hands of France's minister at Philadelphia, that crafty politician the chevalier de La Luzerne. As a result, in June 1781 Congress surrounded Adams with four other peace commissioners, including Franklin, and issued new instructions placing them under the guidance of Vergennes.

Abigail protested strongly to her two close friends in Congress, Lovell and Elbridge Gerry, who had kept her informed of these "diabolical" developments. To join the "unprincipled" Franklin—that "old Sorcerer"—to a man of her husband's integrity threatened the independence of the United States and constituted such a personal insult that he had sufficient cause to resign. But that was exactly what his enemies, Vergennes and La Luzerne, craved, so in the long run she could only advise him to follow his conscience: "You will do what you esteem to be your duty, I doubt not; fearless of consequences, and futurity will discriminate the Honest Man from the Knave tho the present Generation seem little disposed to." Abigail had learned how to counsel John to do what she knew he would. Reinforced by the arrival of John Jay—the only other commissioner to reach Paris in time for the negotiations—the commission skillfully and independently played off England against France, thus demonstrating a mastery of balance of power tactics. As a result, in November 1782 the commissioners secured from Great Britain a preliminary treaty with terms so generous as to amaze Vergennes and assure the independence, territorial integrity, and economic future of the United States. Adams rightfully believed that the peacemakers had contributed as much to the new nation as its generals.

By now the fusion of Abigail's self-image with John's seemed almost total. She fully shared his quest for fame. Her "whole Soul," she admitted, was absorbed in the idea that the "Honour of my dearest Friend, the welfare and happiness of this wide extended Country, ages yet unborn, depend for their happiness and security, upon the able and skillfull, the Honest and upright Discharge of the important trust committed to him." She gloried in his serving the whole nation rather than a single state. "For myself," she explained,

"I have little ambition or pride—for my *Husband* I freely own I have much." His monumental achievements became hers because her sacrifices had made them possible: "I feel a pleasure in being able to sacrifice my selfish passions to the general good, and in imitating the example which has taught me to consider myself and family, but as the small dust of the balance when compaired with the great community." Yes, they might have no fortune in old age, "but let the well earned Fame of having Sacrificed those prospects, from a principal of universal Benevolence and good will to Man, descend as an inheritance to our ofspring." In July 1783 she wrote to John, "I think I feel a greater regard for those persons who love me for your sake, than I should if they Esteemed me on my own account only."

To express her feelings, she referred a correspondent to a favorite letter in *The Spectator* in which a husband paid this tribute to his wife: "she is in love with the immortal part of me, my glory and reputation." Abigail's affection for John Adams now centered on what he prized most highly in himself, his "immortal part," his "glory and reputation." But she took an equal share of credit for his fame: "I will take praise to myself. I feel that it is my due, for having sacrificed so large a portion of my peace and happiness to promote the welfare of my country which I hope for many years to come will reap the benifit, tho it is more than probable unmindfull of the hand that blessed them."

This vicarious relationship with the husband defined but did not devalue the wife's role. Abigail Adams charged American women with the heavy responsibility of stimulating and preserving republican virtue. "America will not wear chains while her daughters are virtuous," she advised a young male friend. She held high hopes that the "Fair Daughters of America" could remain virtuous in this country where matrimony was highly esteemed and where they could marry for love without the European restrictions of class or wealth. But she insisted that the patriotism of women was all the more heroic because they were barred from the public political process:

> Patriotism in the female Sex is the most disinterested of all virtues. Excluded from honours and from offices, we cannot attach ourselves to the State or Government from having held a place of Eminence. Even in the freeest countrys our property is subject to the controul and disposal of our partners, to whom the Laws have given a soverign Authority. Deprived of a voice in Legislation, obliged to submit to those Laws which are imposed upon us, is it not sufficient to make us indifferent to the publick Welfare? Yet all History and every age exhibit Instances of patriotick

virtue in the female Sex; which considering our situation equals the most Heroick of yours.

For her children, and for all American youth, Abigail Adams advocated a reciprocal relationship between the sexes, in which each held a major though different responsibility for the country's future. To avoid England's tragic degeneracy, republican sons and daughters had to guard against the loose principles of *Lord Chesterfield's Letters to His Son,* a popular manual of etiquette and pragmatic morality. On John's advice, Abigail had decided not to read the *Letters* when she first learned of them in 1776. Four years later she did sample them and quickly labeled Chesterfield (Philip Dormer Stanhope) a polished but evil writer, who inculcated the "most immoral, pernicious and Libertine principals" into the minds of youth.

Equally serious, Chesterfield also belittled women, whom he described as merely older children. Despite their "entertaining tattle and sometimes wit," they lacked good sense and reasoning ability. He had never known a woman "who reasoned or acted consequentially for four-and-twenty hours together. A man of sense . . . neither consults them about, nor trusts them with, serious matters." Abigail's response was confident as well as angry: "I could prove to his Lordship were he living that there was one woman in the world who could act consequentially more than 24 hours, since I shall dispise to the end of my days that part of his character." To provide an "Antidote to the poison so profusely administered by this celebrated Letter Writer," she persuaded a Boston newspaper editor to publish a letter written by Mercy Otis Warren warning her son against being "enraptured with Lord Chesterfield."

In spring 1782 a young man reputed to be a disciple of Chesterfield opened a law office in Braintree and took a room with the Cranches. Royall Tyler, Harvard '76, came from a good Boston family and had an ample inheritance. Though he had acquired a reputation for wit and dissipation, he now, at twenty-five, seemed determined to apply himself to his profession. Still, Nabby Adams thought it necessary to warn her cousins Betsy and Lucy Cranch not to be taken in by their lodger's artfulness. She herself had been forbidden even to make Tyler's acquaintance, and she resolved to obey because "our sex cannot be too carefull of the characters of the acquaintance we form."

At seventeen Nabby gave the impression of having willingly and perfectly absorbed her parents' teaching. Appropriately dressed, shyly dignified, and attractively pudgy, she was equally at home in the Braintree cottage or Uncle Smith's

Boston mansion. She had dutifully read the books placed in front of her and had given no hint of rebellion against her parents or the female role. Her conduct with young men seemed unusually discreet and reserved. She was too perfect a daughter to be true. Her lack of sensibility, the favorite eighteenth-century word for emotional capacity, even perplexed her mother at times. The only girl in a family of three boys, the daughter of an absent and romanticized great man and of an overwhelming though loving mother, she had grown into an accommodating woman, with a bland personality, who took seriously her father's admonition to fix her attention "chiefly upon those Virtues and Accomplishments, which contribute the most to qualify Women to act their Parts well in the various Relations of Life, those of Daughter, Sister, Wife, Mother, Friend."

Left to herself, Nabby would likely have kept her resolution to avoid Tyler; but he captivated her mother within a few months. Abigail's mood in 1782 was romantic. The continued absence of a husband in whose achievements she took complete pride led her to reflect on their courtship days with an "undiscrible pleasure." As she came to know Tyler as a person rather than by reputation, she fancied that she saw in his "Sentiments, opinions and actions" a young John

Adams struggling to establish a law practice in Braintree. Soon she opened John's law library to him; then, by the first chill of the winter evenings, this gentleman's "company and conversation" frequently enlivened the Adams fireside. She agreed with Richard Cranch that Tyler's "fine Taste in the Belles Lettres" had helped to develop the minds of the young ladies of their families. In courting the mother he also courted the daughter. In December Abigail wrote two long letters to John in which she reviewed Tyler's background, explained the circumstances of his settling in town, and described his good behavior and legal success. All this was preliminary to reporting a "growing attachment" and predicting that he would win Nabby's heart.

From Paris John expressed shock that his "Princess," fourteen when he had last seen her, should contemplate marriage. He had known Tyler's father and older brother and had no faith that the younger son of this family—a "reformed Rake," so Abigail seemed to describe him— could permanently mend his ways. Mustering his full paternal authority, he forbade his daughter to marry "any Youth upon Earth, who does not totally eradicate every Taste for Gaiety and Expence." He blamed his wife for succumbing to Tyler's "method of Courting Mothers" and for her judgment of Nabby's emotions: "In the

Name of all that is tender dont criticise Your Daughter for those qualities which are her greatest Glory, her Reserve, and her Prudence which I am amazed to hear you call Want of Sensibility. The more Silent She is in Company, the better for me in exact Proportion and I would have this observed as a Rule by the Mother as well as the Daughter." The last was a particularly sore point with him, for he had occasionally been irked with his wife's freedom in expressing herself in mixed company.

Having asserted his male prerogative, John grew uneasy as he realized that he could not judge the case for himself without returning home and abandoning the European mission. Quickly he retreated to giving advice and left the decision to the daughter, mother, and their trusted friends. For reasons of her own—not John's scolding, she made clear—Abigail discouraged any further courtship at present and assured the absent father that Nabby would never marry without his consent. Mother and daughter agreed, though, that Tyler had done nothing to lower their esteem of him and that his affection for Nabby remained undiminished. By the beginning of 1784 John had reconciled himself to the possibility of Nabby's marriage to this "Prodigal Son," but by then the question was intermixed with that of whether Abigail would join him in Europe.

The year 1783 had been filled with indecision. Homesick and weakened by a serious illness, John Adams yearned for Braintree. But his sense of honor had been seriously bruised by the revocation of his former commission to Great Britain; thus he wanted to return from Europe with an irreproachable record. When in September he learned that Congress intended to appoint him, Jay, and Franklin to a new commission to negotiate a commercial treaty with the former mother country, he felt it his duty to accept. At once he urged Abigail to come to him. She received this invitation while mourning her father, dead at seventy-seven. William Smith's passing left Abigail freer to undertake a voyage, but her grief made it difficult to concentrate on that possibility.

In November John grew more insistent, writing, "I cannot be happy, nor tolerable without you." But Abigail pleaded her health, a deadly fear of the North Atlantic in winter, the immodesty of a woman traveling without a male protector, the "awkward figure" she would make in European diplomatic circles, and the irritating congressional indecision. The thought of trying to master the etiquette of royal courts reminded her of what a domestic creature she was. Never in her forty years had she been more than fifty miles from Braintree. Furthermore, she was now certain that Royall Tyler and Nabby, without an open courtship, had reached a confidential agreement to marry as soon as they received her father's approval. Tyler had purchased one of the town's fine homes with this object in mind. Abigail neither wanted the couple to marry at once—she did not yet know that John had resigned himself to that possibility—nor to leave Nabby behind unmarried.

Early in the new year Abigail pushed her fears aside; she would go and take Nabby with her. A separation would test the strength of Tyler's affection as well as the permanence of his reformation. This plan pleased both parents; but Nabby, uncertain of her own mind, agreed to go out of "necessity" rather than by her own "choice." Charles and Tommy would continue their education at Haverhill with the Shaws. Uncle Tufts was willing to assume responsibility for the house and farm, and sister Mary promised to take Abigail's place in caring for John's mother, still living in the adjacent cottage (John's birthplace). As for servants, she would take two: a man from Josiah Quincy's household and a maid from her own home.

Uncle Smith urged Abigail to leave on a vessel departing late in April, but she delayed, hoping to have a letter from John, from whom she had not heard since November. She feared she might

pass him on the high seas after he had suddenly
changed plans. When no letter arrived, she
booked passage on a sturdy merchantman, the
Active, whose captain planned to sail for England in the middle of June. By this time she knew
that Congress had finally acted: Adams,
Franklin, and Jefferson (replacing Jay) were
commissioned to negotiate commercial treaties
with a number of nations. Hastening to his new
assignment, Jefferson reached Boston on June
18, hoping to escort to France the wife of his
good friend. It was too late; the *Active* would
sail in a day or two and Abigail could not
change her plans.

Charles and Tommy came for a last visit.
Then on Friday, June 18, Abigail said a tearful
and exhausting farewell to her many Braintree
relatives and neighbors before riding to Boston
with sister Mary. On Saturday her baggage was
put on board, and Sunday at noon a carriage
took her to Rowe's Wharf, where "100 Gentlemen," she estimated, had gathered to pay their
respects. She was quickly ushered aboard and
the *Active* got under way at once, its course set
for England.

In a letter to Johnny a few weeks before, she
commented that as a girl she had earnestly desired to see the mother country, but her sex
and station in life had afforded not "the least

prospect of gratifying that inclination." Now to her astonishment, a mighty Revolution and her marriage to one of its "principal Characters" had put her on a ship headed to "that once great Nation."

VI

"The Amaizing Difference"

1784–1785

The *Active* had been under way only a few hours before Mrs. Adams agreed fully with her husband that the high seas were no place for a lady. For the first ten days of the voyage she suffered almost constantly from seasickness. The "horrid dirtiness of the ship," its "laizy dirty Negro" cook, and the fumes given off by the cargo of oil and potash increased her nausea. Water from the deck leaked into the cabins to wash vomit and other slop across the floor. She could do little but lie in her cabin, where the door opening upon the men's quarters was the only source of air. With her servants and the other women passengers too ill to nurse her, she depended totally upon male strangers for even the most intimate services. "It is impossible," she lamented in her journal, "to preserve that Decency and Cleanliness which ought to be an inherint principal in every female." She gave thanks that John could not see her in such a condition.

By the first of July the seas calmed and nearly everyone recovered from seasickness. Her health and spirits revived, Abigail found that she "might reign mistress on board without any offence," for the captain, though an "admirable seaman," concerned himself with little except seamanship. The housewife in her took over, and she ordered her manservant and some of the crew below to scrape the cabin floors and scour them with vinegar until the boards reappeared, to the great gratitude of her fellow passengers. Furthermore, she took the liberty of instructing the cook and preparing some puddings herself. Thereafter the voyage proved more tolerable, even though the dampness and the chill Atlantic air brought a recurrence of her rheumatism. Despite the motion of the ship, she managed to read and write. Her letters and journal took the measure of the other passengers, noting particularly that their literary knowledge seldom matched hers. For appropriate reading she turned to a popular manual of home medicine, perhaps remembering that one reason for this trip was to nurse John back to health. As she neared the English coast on a gentle sea after a generally favorable voyage of a month, her spirits soared.

A fierce gale in the English Channel drove the ship up the coast past Dover to an anchorage off the small town of Deal. After three sleepless nights and a "voilent sick head ack," Abigail willingly joined those who accepted the offer of local pilots to put them ashore through the six-foot surf. Each in the embrace of a man, mother and daughter managed to keep from falling overboard until the waves tossed their small boat broadside on the beach. Like nymphs "just rising from the Sea," they trudged across the wet, soft sand to a nearby inn. Soaked and weary, Abigail Adams had reached the land of her ancestors, the former mother country. Her indoctrination into European ways came quickly. When their baggage came ashore, she had to hire a separate porter to carry each piece of luggage "only a few steps" to the custom-house and then another to return each to the inn.

The next morning the party from the ship set off for London in post chaises. Those seventy-two miles gave Abigail her first glimpses of England and its people. She was impressed by the intensive cultivation of the land, the massive "old

Gothick Cathedrals," the estates of the aristocracy, and the prompt, polite services provided by
inns along the way. She was shocked, however,
at the callousness of people toward a "poor
wretch" captured after a robbery. Her countrymen, she invidiously noted, would have at least
commiserated with an unfortunate man who
must hang for his crime.

At eight that evening (July 21) they entered
London and stopped at a hotel. From an American friend they learned that Johnny had waited a
month for their arrival but had returned disappointed to The Hague. There was nothing to do
but take "more private" lodgings and await further word. Abigail had brought few clothes with
her. Now she had to submit to the "tyranny of
fashion" by using the service of "the staymaker,
the mantua maker, the hoop maker, the shoe
maker, the miliner and hair dresser, all of whom
are necessary to transform one into the fashionable Lady." Not impressed with the dress of
English women, Abigail decided to purchase as
little as possible until she reached Paris, where
she anticipated that it would be more "necessary
to conform to the fashion." So ecstatic was John
at word of their safe arrival that he wrote from
The Hague for them to buy all the "proper"
clothing, "let the Expence be what it will." Elizabeth Quincy Smith would have been proud to

see her daughter and granddaughter adapt to the fashion of Europe while maintaining—they believed—the "purity and simplicity of manners" becoming to virtuous republican women.

Mother and daughter were welcomed to London by numerous Americans, many of them homesick loyalists eager for news from the native land they might never see again. Ten or a dozen a day came calling, and there were endless invitations to dine. There was time, too, to see the sights; yet not even Westminster Abbey or Alexander Pope's garden at Twickenham attracted Abigail more than the studio of John Singleton Copley, the Boston artist who had moved to England on the eve of the Revolution. The year before, John Adams had commissioned Copley to paint his portrait in commemoration of the successful peace negotiations. Now Abigail viewed the finished work and described it to her sisters: "I have been to see a very Elegant picture of Mr. Adams which belongs to Mr. Copely, and was taken by him. It is a larg full length picture. He is drawn with a Globe before him; the Map of Europe in his hand and at a distance 2 female figures representing Innocence and Peace." She added of the man she had not seen for over four and one-half years, "It is said to be an admirable likeness." Here on canvas she saw the husband for whose fame she had sacrificed much of their

married life, the absent father she had romanticized to their children. This "most beautiful
painting" of an aristocratic John Adams settling
the affairs of the world provided a measure of
emotional compensation for the lonely years of
the last two decades.

Johnny rushed back to London from The
Hague and on July 30 embraced his mother and
sister in a warm reunion. Abigail had sent a boy
to Europe in 1779; now she beheld a man she
could hardly believe to be her son. On August 7
John reached London. Abigail could never bring
herself to describe what she felt on this day of
which she had so often dreamed. Some scenes, she
believed, surpassed even the ability of the poet or
artist to depict. But John knew the perfect gift for
the occasion: Samuel Johnson's *Lives of the Poets*.

Early the next morning they set out for Paris,
the family riding in their handsome coach, "second hand, but good as if new," a bargain Johnny
had bought from an English gentleman. The two
American servants followed in a hired post
chaise. At three that afternoon they embarked at
Dover and landed in Calais after an all-night
channel crossing. They took four leisurely days
to travel the two hundred miles to Paris, stopping along the way to view such curiosities as
the estate of the prince de Condé, who kept 150
hunting dogs, had built palatial stables for 240

horses, and maintained a theater in which he himself acted. Yet both Nabby and her mother recorded their disappointment with what they first saw of France—poor villages, dirty streets, mean houses, ragged and indifferent peasants, women at work in the fields, and crudely harnessed horses. And when they entered Paris on August 13, Abigail pronounced it the "very dirtiest place" she had ever seen, a town she knew first through the nose rather than the eyes.

After a few days in a hotel, the family moved to Auteuil, a village four miles along the road to Versailles and near Franklin's residence at Passy. Among Auteuil's villas of the rich and famous stood the Hôtel Rouhault, which Commissioner Adams had rented from the comte de Rouhault. This large house had acquired notoriety earlier in the century as the site of the scandalous amours of two actresses. Adams had come to know it while convalescing there the year before as the guest of its former tenants. Auteuil pleased him because it was sufficiently "distant from the putrid Streets of Paris" and adjoined the Bois de Boulogne, a royal forest where he loved to walk. The house overlooked the river Seine, and its rear windows and doors opened on a five-acre formal garden. Two months after she had ridden away from her saltbox cottage in Braintree, Abigail Adams was mistress of a French villa with room for forty beds.

Here she lived for nine interesting months. The joy of being reunited with her husband and eldest son, and a sense of duty as the wife of an American statesman, overcame any doubts concerning her ability to cope with a foreign culture.

First came the task of settling their domestic affairs. Sections of the house and garden were in disrepair, but the salon and dining room on the first floor and the family's chambers on the second were magnificent. It had been prohibitively expensive to bring to France the furnishings from John's house at The Hague, so Abigail had to purchase china, plate, glassware, linen, and other necessities. She discovered that French servants—"Lazy Wretches" she called them at first—considered themselves specialists: "one will not touch what belongs to the business of another." Thus it required at least eight merely to get by. She was torn between the fears that Americans would think them extravagant and that the miserliness of Congress toward its diplomats would make her country appear ridiculous. Congress had recently reduced the salaries of the commissioners, which could be paid, if at all, only from the loan John had secured from Holland. She contrasted her household with that of the Spanish ambassador, who had seventy servants, or the English ambassador with fifty. With Johnny's assistance, she kept careful accounts of expenditures; but these only convinced her that John's station obliged them, for the sake of appearance, "to eat and drink up" all they had. As much as ever, their financial worries were left to her. Toward the end of their stay in France, she wrote to Dr. Tufts with pride but also perhaps a touch of resentment: "Mr A[dams] has been so long a Statesman that I cannot get him to think enough upon his domestick affairs. He loves to have every Thing as it should be, but does not wish to be troubled about them. He chuses I should write and think about them and give directions. Tho I am very willing to relieve him from every care in my power, yet I think it has too much the appearance of wielding instead of sharing the Scepter."

Managing her greatly expanded household proved far easier for Abigail than learning to feel at home in French society. She could read the language but made only slow progress in speaking it. To instruct the servants she mixed English with simple French. Going into society without husband or son to interpret was another matter; and she discovered that strangers were expected to make the first call, an awkward procedure for one unable to converse.

Her first meeting with a French woman of quality dampened her desire to meet others. On September 1 the family dined at Franklin's, where the guests included Madame Helvétius, the rich widow of the philosopher Claude-Adrien Helvétius. The salon in her home in Auteuil near the Adamses attracted men of science and letters, among them Franklin, who loved her dearly and had at one time proposed marriage to her. Though John had often written of the old doctor's dalliance with French women, Abigail was unprepared for a face-to-face encounter with Madame Helvétius. Madame "entered the room with a careless, jaunty air; upon seeing ladies who were strangers to her, she bawled out [in French], 'Ah! mon Dieu, where is Franklin? Why did you not tell me there were ladies here?' " Abigail knew that Madame Helvétius had once been a handsome woman, but now her decayed beauty was matched by her slovenly dress. Over frizzled hair "she had a small straw hat, with a dirty gauze half-handkerchief round it, and a bit of dirtier gauze . . . was bowed on behind." When Franklin entered the room, she "gave him a double kiss, one upon each cheek, and another upon his forehead." At dinner she sat between Franklin and John Adams, "frequently locking her hand into the Doctor's, and sometimes spreading her arms upon the backs of both the gentlemen's chairs, then throwing her arm carelessly upon the Doctor's neck."

Franklin had told Abigail that this lady was "a genuine Frenchwoman, wholly free from affectation or stiffness of behaviour, and one of the best women in the world." But the Braintree matron quickly "set her down for a very bad one, although sixty years of age, and a widow." After dinner, Madame Helvétius reclined upon a settee, "where she showed more than her feet. She had a little lap-dog, who was, next to the Doctor, her favorite. This she kissed, and when he wet the floor she wiped it up with her chemise." Disgusted, Abigail wished for no "acquaintance with any ladies of this cast."

Not until she met the marquise de Lafayette two months later did Abigail lower her guard against French womanhood. The wife of this hero of the American Revolution was friendly, unaffected, able to speak some English, and— most striking of all—plainly dressed. They exchanged numerous visits. Abigail listened with understanding as Madame Lafayette recounted her life story: given a husband in an arranged marriage before she "was capable of Love," she had nevertheless devoted her life to him and to their family. As a result she was far happier than those French women of her class who sought pleasure outside the home in "dissipation and amusement." In time both Abigail and her daughter commented favorably on the "ease and softness" in the manners of well-bred, educated French women. And Abigail noticed with disgust that some of the American women, not possessed of these inbred qualities, crudely attempted to imitate the Parisians. Her admiration for those educated females who could command the intellectual respect of distinguished men grew during her short stay in France.

Abigail readily recognized that one soon grew accustomed to what in the beginning seemed strange in a foreign culture. For the first time in her life she entered a theater and discovered that she was fond of plays and operas, particularly if they were based on literature she had read or could now read. Yet at the initial sight of thinly dressed female dancers exposing their legs on the stage, she felt her "delicacy wounded" and was "ashamed to be seen to look at them." But she candidly confessed in a letter to her sister: "Shall I speak a truth, and say that repeatedly seeing these dances has worn off that disgust, which I at first felt, and that I see them now with pleasure?" She retreated quickly, however, into a homily on the offstage immorality of the dancing girls.

After recoiling in horror at the crime and prostitution of London's streets, she had been pleased to discover that by contrast Paris seemed

a city of law and order. Then she learned that behind this facade of decency there were 52,000
registered prostitutes. With Nabby she visited
the Enfants Trouvés, a well-ordered royal or-
phanage where the Sisters of Charity unques-
tioningly accepted unwanted babies around the
clock, averaging six thousand admissions a year.
She had been "credibly inform'd that one half of
the Children annually born in that immense City
of Paris" were *enfants trouvés*. What a comparison, she exclaimed, of this "Country grown old
in Debauchery and lewdness" to that virtuous
young republic where marriage was "holy and
honourable," where most children were raised
by industrious, sober parents, and where the law
required those responsible for illegitimate children to do their duty!

"If you ask me what is the Business of Life
here," she wrote to Mercy Otis Warren, "I answer
Pleasure." She marveled that in this society "to be
triste is a complaint of a most serious Nature,"
and she blamed Catholicism for such an attitude
toward life. The ease with which forgiveness
could be had in the confessional, she believed,
produced a light-hearted view of sin. On Sunday
the Bois de Boulogne, within earshot of the
Adams residence, was filled with "Musick and
Dancing, jollity and Mirth of every kind," and
even booths selling food, drink, and a variety of

merchandise. By contrast, she and the family visited different churches, coming closest to duplicating that of Braintree in the chapel of the Dutch ambassador, where Calvinism was preached in its original French. In Passy at the villa of Ferdinand Grand, banker to the commissioners, Abigail found an oasis in a Catholic society. The home of these Swiss Protestants displayed the "Decorum and Decency of Manners," the "conjugal and family affection," which she regarded as marks of her own faith. By contrast, the celibacy of so many men and women in clerical orders tended to debase the institution of marriage. Still, all of the Adamses enjoyed the company of the three abbés living in Auteuil. Abigail's strictures on Catholicism were always general, not personal.

She was sadly mistaken in her judgment of one famous Protestant she met in France. Both mother and daughter fell completely under the spell of the ambassador from Sweden, the baron de Staël-Holstein. Here in real life, Abigail explained to her niece, was a man such as she imagined Sir Charles Grandison to be. His fine figure and commanding countenance prejudiced her in his favor at first sight. He complimented Nabby on her angelic skin and Abigail on her wittiness, leaving both utterly charmed. The baron dined with the Adamses at least once, and they attended a sumptuous dinner party at his "Grand Hotel," where everything was the most elegant Abigail had ever seen. She did not learn until later that de Staël had been a penniless adventurer who had capitalized on his charm to win the support of both his king and the queen of France in a long campaign to contract a marriage of state to Germaine Necker, the daughter of an extremely wealthy Swiss-French family. Their loveless marriage gave the name of Madame de Staël to the remarkable woman whose writings and amours became the sensation of Napoleonic Europe.

As she observed French gentlemen devoting their lives to pleasure, Abigail gave more thought to the future of her own sons. Letters from Haverhill reported that Charles and Tommy were healthy and devoted to their studies. In addition, sister Elizabeth had enrolled them in a dancing school where both did "excellently, but Mr. Charles exquisitely." It was no comfort to his mother to learn that Charles, nearly ready for college, was the favorite partner of the girls in the quarterly balls given by the dancing master. Already she worried that his "disposition, and sensibility would render him more liable to female attachments." About her eldest son, the "Young Hercules," as she styled John Quincy, she had no such worries. He was at present "much better occupied with his Horace and Tacitus." Yet he was lonesome for friends of his own age and eager to begin college. His parents agreed that a republican youth of his promise should not risk the corrupting influence of a European education, and they made plans for him to sail home in the spring.

Meanwhile the Adamses prepared to move to England. The commissioners had met with no success in concluding the all-important commercial treaty with Great Britain and had advised a new plan of diplomatic representation. Their friend John Jay, now in charge of congressional foreign affairs, agreed wholeheartedly. Early in May came word that Adams had been appointed minister to Britain and Jefferson to France.

Franklin, approaching eighty and suffering from a painful ailment, would return to Pennsylvania. Despite their earlier bitterness toward him, both John and Abigail had maintained an outwardly cordial relationship with the venerable philosopher. Though she acknowledged that he had "always been vastly social and civil" to her, she never forgave him for his support of Vergennes against her husband. She harbored the notion that these intrigues, which had led Congress to revoke John's original commission as peace negotiator, were responsible for Britain's present stubbornness toward her former colonies. Time, however, had given Abigail a "little sweet and innocent revenge," for now Franklin's salary was being paid from the Dutch loan that he had advised John not to negotiate.

Leaving Jefferson brought no mixed feelings. Her affection for this widower of her own age had grown steadily during their months together, especially as she consoled him on the recent loss of his wife and cared for him during an illness his first winter in France. The Virginian had probably never before known a woman so nearly his intellectual equal with whom he could discuss such topics as literature and foreign policy, as well as the proper management of a household. He had even attempted to ease her dislike of slavery by insisting that slaves in Virginia were so well treated that their numbers grew faster than the whites. Not entirely convinced, she still described him as an "excellent Man, Worthy of his Nation," and "one of the choice ones of the earth." The new diplomatic arrangement denied her, as she put it, the "increasing pleasure and intimacy which a longer acquaintance with a respected Friend promised." He had responded to her in kind. She is, he later wrote Madison, "one of most estimable characters on earth." Johnny echoed his mother's sentiments when he observed in the diary he had begun to keep, "Spent the evening with Mr. Jefferson whom I love to be with, because he is a man of very extensive learning and pleasing manners." Future political battles would not entirely destroy the affectionate friendship between Abigail Adams and Thomas Jefferson that began in France.

Mother and daughter filled their last weeks in France with activities they never expected to repeat. They joined the "Promenade à Longchamp," the rite of spring in which Parisians turned Holy Week into a display of fine clothes and carriages. But Abigail "could not help feeling foolish" as they rode in the funeral-like procession for the sole purpose of seeing and being seen. More rewarding was a Te Deum at Notre Dame cathedral, sung in the presence of the king in thanksgiving for the birth of a prince. Farewells to diplomatic and personal friends, a visit to Versailles, and a final tour of Paris took her past the middle of May. Despite her reservations concerning French religion and culture, she now began to understand what was meant by the "observation that nobody ever leaves paris but with a degree of tristeness [*tristesse,* or sadness]."

Johnny had already gone. Abigail's sadness over his departure was increased by regrets at leaving her house at Auteuil, where the garden was just beginning to show its beauty in a pleasant spring. On May 20 the Adams family set out for England, surprised and heartened that their French domestics seemed moved at the farewell. They traveled leisurely toward the coast, while they pored over Jefferson's recently published *Notes on the State of Virginia* which he gave them as a farewell gift. "It is our Meditation all the Day long," wrote John; its passages on the demoralizing influence of slavery on whites are "worth Diamonds." Nonetheless, the irrepressible Abigail offered a correction. She and Nabby thought Jefferson had erred in not including in his list of American geniuses their two favorite painters, Copley and Benjamin West.

France had left both superficial and profound marks on Abigail Adams. An increased sophistication in dress, manners, and household furnishings would be conspicuous for the remainder of her life. Her confidence in herself as a person had been bolstered by the many opportunities to test her mind and values in the intellectual and social capital of Europe. Those nine months in France had, at the same time they enlarged her world view, confirmed her faith in the political culture of republican America. Never before had she understood the "amazing difference which subsists between those Countries which have passt the Zenith of their glory, saped by Luxery, and undermined by the rage for pleasure and a Young, a flourishing, a free, and I may add a virtuous

Country uncontrouled by a Royal Mandate, un-shackled by a military police, unfearfull of the thundring anathamas of Ecclesiastic power, where every individual possest of industry and probity, has a sure reward for his Labour, unin-fested with thousands of useless Virmin whom Luxery supports upon the Bread of Idleness, a Country where Virtue is still revered: and modesty still Cloaths itself in crimson."

VII

"I Will Not Strike My Colours"

1785–1788

The Adamses rode into London with their heads high. They came not as the first minister and his wife from the thirteen loosely united states that had won independence thanks to the European balance of power and now had the audacity to demand commercial concessions from the mother country they had renounced. No, John Adams saw himself as the representative of a victorious republic whose soldiers and statesmen had shown what a virtuous, liberty-loving people could accomplish. In England he faced the crucial test of the post-Revolutionary strength of the United States. Furthermore, he could expect to be the target for the accumulated hostility of English Tories and exiled American loyalists.

Abigail felt the demands of this assignment fully as much as John. For the first time since her husband had become a major public figure, she shared at close range the rewards and frustrations of his career. In London she participated daily in the cares of his office, freed him from domestic concerns, softened the intensity of his moods, and bolstered his frequently bruised ego. She became an insightful observer of his associates, a confidential sounding board for his ideas, and an energetic private defender of his reputation. Their truly reciprocal roles burdened them equally.

Reaching London on May 26, the family took temporary quarters at a hotel. At once John delivered his credentials to the foreign minister and on June 1 was formally presented to George III. It was an emotional encounter for both: the Revolutionary leader face to face with the king who had stubbornly resisted American independence. The unexpected respect and civility he received from the monarch augured well for his mission, so John tried to convince himself. He could now appear at court with the other ministers and present his secretary of legation, Colonel William Stephens Smith.

Then came the turn of the ladies. Abigail unhappily learned that she would be expected to appear frequently at the queen's receptions held weekly during most of the year. "You cannot go twice the same season in the same dress," she complained, "and a Court dress you cannot make use of anywhere else." Nevertheless, late in June mother and daughter dutifully made their entry to the palace. They dressed, as Abigail had decided befitted republican women in this situation, in the elegant fashion of the court but as plainly as that style would permit. They stood for more than four hours in the drawing room while the royal family moved around a circle of two hundred guests, making inane small talk with each. The king greeted Mrs. Adams pleasantly with a kiss on the cheek, but the queen received her stiffly, with obvious embarrassment.

Abigail suffered some pangs of her republican conscience during the ceremony. She reflected that she must look like a fool to stand so dressed until nearly exhausted only "to be spoken to by royalty." Yet the experience was not without its reward, for she found those at court to be "like the rest of Mankind, mere Men and Women." She left "quite Self Satisfied" and with renewed confidence: "tho I could not boast of making an appearence in point of person or richness of attire, . . . yet I know I will not strike my colours to Many of them."

During her years in London, Abigail appeared at court from time to time, at least making certain to be seen on special occasions such as royal birthdays and anniversaries of the coronation. She derived little pleasure from these functions and resolved not to give the queen any more opportunities of "displaying her Airs" than duty demanded. She did, though, enjoy one moment of triumph at court. In a crowded drawing room during February 1786, she presented to the king and queen Mrs. William Bingham, the young wife of a rich Philadelphian noted for her beauty. All eyes followed her and whispers of "Is she an American?" passed through the room. Abigail was so proud to see an American lady acknowledged to be elegant and beautiful at the Court of Saint James that she momentarily forgave Mrs. Bingham her extravagance in preparing for this presentation.

With John at once overloaded with work, Abigail had spent her first two weeks in London hunting for a house. There were few dwellings both appropriate for a minister from a sovereign nation and available at a price he could afford. But at last she found one in Grosvenor Square that answered the purpose. Though modest, it was pleasantly situated in this unusually large square bordered by fine houses (one of them Lord North's) and near parks in which to walk and ride. The center of the square featured a beautifully landscaped circle lighted at night by dozens of lamps. John sent for the furnishings from his house at The Hague, and by the first week in July the Adamses had gone to house-keeping again.

Living in London severely taxed Abigail's managerial ability. Wages and prices were higher than in Paris. Told that her house required at least eleven servants, she resolved to get by with eight, including the two liveried footmen who waited on the table, answered the door, and rode behind the carriage. As in France, there existed a rigid hierarchy among English servants, and no one, however unoccupied, would touch the work of another. By such a system, she under-stood, the English nobility supported more of the poor; yet it galled her to pay wages to ser-vants idle much of the day. Vendors pressed their services upon her with recommendations from noble customers and offers of liberal credit. But she ran the household on a strictly cash basis. The fear of personal debt haunted both Abigail and John.

Consequently, the American legation would not be noted for a sumptuous table. Abigail much preferred small informal dinners with the family and Colonel Smith, a permanent boarder, and with a few visiting Americans. A Virginian who had dined with the Adamses recorded in his diary that "dinner was plain, neat, and good." He added that "Mrs. Adams's accomplishments and agreeableness" would have more than compensated for anything lacking in the quality of the food. When John first entertained his fellow ministers, Abigail fed them with a "noble turtle, weighing a hundred and fourteen pounds," the gift of an American sea captain. She ordered special tables built for this occasion, purchased new table linen, supervised the other preparations, and then took Nabby visiting to leave John alone with his all-male dinner party. Though she regarded it as unhealthy, she resigned herself to the local custom of eating only two meals a day, a late breakfast and dinner some time between four and six. Both she and John grew fatter on this regimen, apparently from overeating because of the longer interval between meals.

Despite her endeavor to take a flexible attitude toward foreign customs, Abigail never felt at home in English social circles. She met too much form and too little of the sincere and warm-hearted social intercourse on which she had thrived in her homeland. Paying and receiving calls became a dull duty. Many parties consisted of nothing more than a greeting from the hostess, who then seated her guest at a card table with strangers to gamble the evening away. "Good Heavens!" she exclaimed to Mary Cranch, "were reasonable beings made for this?" She avoided the card table whenever possible; however, when play was unavoidable—so she observed with a touch of republican pride—her luck was usually good, even against experts. In gatherings of women Abigail felt alone. At mixed parties she preferred the conversation and attention of the gentlemen to those of the ladies. Only a magnificent assemblage, such as the grand ball given by the French ambassador, could excite her interest in London social life.

Abigail's close friends were nearly all Americans. For the first few months she enjoyed the company of Elizabeth Temple, daughter of the Massachusetts statesman James Bowdoin. During the next year, Abigail Rogers, wife of a Boston merchant, became Abigail's dearest companion. Good friends, though not as close, were the Copleys and the wife of the American painter Benjamin West. Other Americans streamed through the legation, but after Mrs. Rogers left in 1786 Abigail had little opportunity for the intimacy she craved with like-minded women.

The Massachusetts refugees in London created a distressing problem for the Adamses. Abigail favored permitting repentant loyalists to return home, and she sympathized deeply with those refugee wives whom she regarded as the innocent victims of their husbands' mistaken politics. Some she had known well in Boston before the war. Yet attempts to renew old acquaintances proved awkward at best and humiliating at worst. It was difficult to visit a friendly loyalist without encountering others totally unrepentant and venting their resentment toward anyone associated with the new nation. For one, Harrison Gray, the pre-Revolutionary treasurer of Massachusetts, talked loudly about the desirability of hanging John Adams. The press greeted the arrival of the American minister with squibs ridiculing him and the country he represented. Abigail attributed much of this scurrility to spiteful refugees, and she supported John's policy of not replying even to barefaced lies.

Aside from such unpleasantness, Abigail's three years in England provided a rich educational experience that revealed how much she, though past forty, could still grow in mind and spirit. Hearing Handel's *Messiah* performed in Westminster Abbey by six hundred voices thrilled this New Englander whose church would still not permit an organ. During the "Hallelujah Chorus," she wrote later, "I could scarcly believe myself an inhabitant of Earth. I wore[?] one continued shudder from the beginning to the end of the performance."

Sunday became her favorite day of the week. The family seldom missed driving the six miles to the dissenting chapel at Hackney to hear Dr. Richard Price. Moral philosopher and mathematician as well as preacher, Price's outspoken support of the colonial cause had won the esteem of American leaders. After the Revolution he yielded to no republican in the belief that the hope of the world rested on the United States. But, like the Adamses, he worried lest vice and luxury destroy that hope, and he continued to warn in print against such a possibility. By sheer force of intellect and personality, this descendant of Puritans now commanded the respect even of George III's top ministers. Though Price was far from being an orator, Abigail wrote that she "would willingly go much further to hear a Man so liberal so sensible and so good as he is. He has a Charity which embraces all Mankind and a benevolence which would do good to all of them. His Subjects are instructive and edifying."

Abigail found in Price's sermons the consummation of her deep faith. He brought reason and science to bear on religion without rejecting the role of providence in human affairs, but neither did he insist on theological dogma such as the doctrine of the Trinity. She especially appreciated a sermon on marriage that stressed the relative duties of husband and wife. She was capable, nonetheless, of twisting his teaching toward her own views. After a powerful sermon on universal brotherhood, she recalled that Price had urged the Christian to prefer "virtue more than consanguinity." She then concluded that "now upon this principal I believe I ought to love my Countrymen best, as I really think them possest of a larger portion of virtue than any other Nation, I am acquainted with." Price became a personal friend, as did Joseph Priestley, the chemist who had discovered oxygen but was now more interested in theology and political reform.

In England, as in France, the theater challenged Abigail's cultural heritage. It took her only a performance or two to decide that the English stage, where the actors overshadowed the plays, did not appeal to her as much as the French. And she could still not reconcile herself to the sight of female dancers or acrobats in short skirts, however well clad underneath. After seeing a performer thus dressed do a headstand, she wrote, "I can never look upon a Woman in such Situations, without conceiving all that adorns and Beautifies the female Character, delicacy modesty and diffidence, as wholly laid aside, and nothing of the Woman but the Sex left."

Then in the fall of 1785 one woman transformed the theater for Abigail. Mrs. Sarah Siddons, the most celebrated actress of the age, played Desdemona in Shakespeare's *Othello*. Abigail managed to secure tickets, and she and Nabby took their seats in the Drury Lane Theatre with great expectations at the prospect of seeing the woman who was the toast of a nation. The evening proved both exciting and disturbing. Mrs. Siddons's cleverly concealed pregnancy did not trouble Abigail as much as seeing the black Othello make love to the fair heroine: "She was interesting beyond any actress I had ever seen; but I lost much of the pleasure of the play, from the sooty appearance of the Moor. Perhaps it may be early prejudice; but I could not separate the African color from the man, nor prevent that disgust and horror which filled my mind every time I saw him touch the gentle Desdemona; nor did I wonder that Brabantio thought some love potion or some witchcraft had been practised to make his daughter fall in love with what she scarcely dared to look upon."

After seeing Mrs. Siddons in several other plays, Abigail became a warm admirer. She did not, though, agree with the critics that Lady Macbeth was Siddons's finest role but considered her "too great to be put in so detestable a character." Abigail could not separate the player from her judgment of the play; she dared even to offer the opinion that too much of Shakespeare's language was uncouth and required editing for the stage.

She admired the actress most as a woman who had achieved greatness while preserving an unblemished character. The leading man in Siddons's plays was always her brother; thus "both her husband and the virtuous part of the audience can see them in the tenderest scenes without once fearing for their reputation." Moreover, as the mother of five children and the wife of an actor of good character, Mrs. Siddons combined the accepted female role with a brilliant public career.

The more Abigail learned of current knowledge and observed examples of female genius, the more she deplored the failure to educate American women. In 1787 she subscribed to a series of twelve lectures on natural science. Illness prevented her from attending more than five, but these (on electricity, magnetism, hydrostatics, optics, and pneumatics) were "an assemblage of Ideas entirely new" to her. She wrote to a niece that "it was like going into a beautifull Country, which I never saw before, a Country which our American Females are not permitted to visit or inspect." Since in the United States science was taught only in colleges closed to women, she feared she would never have the opportunity to learn what she had missed in the other seven lectures. She was willing to grant the male dogma that the household was "the peculiar province of the Female Character." Yet she still insisted that women were "rational Beings," and thus their reason "might with propriety receive the highest possible cultivation." Though the educated female could expect "to draw upon herself the jealousy of the Men and the envy of the Women," Abigail saw no "way to remedy this evil but by increasing the number of accomplished women" to break the masculine monopoly of education.

A new portrait confirmed the strength of Abigail Adams's mind and spirit. Soon after moving to England the family sat for Mather Brown, a young American painter studying in London. His portrait of Abigail at forty—"a good likeness" according to Nabby—was striking. The large, assertive eyes dominated all else. Her face radiated confident firmness, and the tight-lipped smile of the young bride in the 1766 pastel had given way to a pleasant earnestness. Handsomely but not ostentatiously dressed, she was a model of her own standards of genteel republican womanhood.

The daughter's portrait resembled the mother's scarcely at all. Nabby's face had the bland, uncertain quality of her father's. There was nothing captivating about it, and the fashionable clothes seemed more vital than the woman who wore them. This portrait suggested why Abigail still apologized for Nabby's "Native reserve" and described her as a "very silent Character." Brown captured on canvas the contrast between mother and daughter at the very time Nabby faced the most critical question of her young life.

Her trial separation from Royall Tyler went well at first. With John reconciled to the match, Abigail had few doubts that in time her only daughter would marry Tyler. He had requested the mother to correspond with him, and she gladly obliged. Her first letter, written on shipboard, advised him how he should conduct himself during the separation. Nabby wrote regularly and received a few letters from him. The couple exchanged miniature portraits of each other, and Tyler thanked her father for consenting to the engagement. All seemed settled. At the beginning of 1785, Abigail closed a letter to her intended son-in-law with words of assurance: "I view you with more confidence as the person to whose care and protection I shall one day resign a beloved and only Daughter."

Early in 1785 Nabby had a short note from Tyler, then nothing more for months. The daughter suffered in silence, for no one wanted to raise the painful subject. Nabby wrote a letter of reproof, and her parents began the slow process of making discreet inquiries by mail. The early suspicions, which they had hoped to bury forever, now surfaced again. His inexplicable conduct seemed especially dishonorable when compared with the behavior of the model gentleman who dined daily with the family and attempted to cheer Nabby during her disappointment.

William Stephens Smith was the son of a prosperous New York merchant. After graduation from Princeton in 1774, he had studied law before joining the Continental Army, in which he had commanded a regiment while in his early twenties and served honorably under several generals, including Lafayette and Washington. As a reward, Congress had appointed him secretary to the London legation. Abigail liked Colonel Smith from the beginning, judging him "a Man of an independent Spirit, high and strict sentiments of honour, [and] Much the Gentleman in his manners and address." Also in his favor, he had declined active membership in the Society of the Cincinnati, the order of Revolutionary officers that John Adams feared would turn into a hereditary nobility. Thirty and handsome—"tall, slender and a good figure," Abigail described him—Colonel Smith charmed both mother and daughter with his dinner table talk, his reading aloud from their favorite authors, and his gallantry as an escort to theaters and other public places. After a few weeks his growing attachment to Nabby became so obvious that he had to be told of her engagement. His response was in keeping with the character Abigail had ascribed to him, for he promised to stay out of Nabby's way in the future. As if to show his sincerity, he asked for a short leave of absence to attend a military review in Prussia.

While Smith traveled, Nabby broke off her engagement to Tyler. Her parents concurred gladly after reading a letter from Mary Cranch describing his erratic behavior. A brilliant career lay ahead for Tyler as a Vermont jurist and a major contributor to American literature of the post-Revolutionary generation. But in 1785 his ambivalence at the prospect of settling down left him unable to act the part expected of him. And some of the attraction for him of the Adams cottage had been the mother, a consideration that he may have faced for the first time when left alone to sort out his feelings. In any case, Tyler could find no way to break the engagement gracefully or even honorably. His embarrassment led to conduct that, duly reported to London by their relatives, made the family thankful to be rid of him. When at last he wrote to Nabby in an effort to excuse his neglect, she refused to answer; but her mother did. Tyler never replied.

Without informing the Adamses of his whereabouts, Smith overstayed his leave by remaining in Europe for four months in the company of a Latin American adventurer. In view of the burden of work left to Minister Adams, his secretary's absence was inexcusable. Yet somehow the colonel charmed his way back into the good graces of the family. After some weeks the news of the broken engagement slipped out, and he pressed his suit vigorously. Once sure of the daughter, he wooed the mother and through her obtained the father's blessing. Abigail was delighted but saw no reason for them to rush into matrimony, especially in view of their limited finances. Smith persisted, nonetheless, joking that soldiers courted more rapidly than men not accustomed to storming citadels. Nabby left the matter entirely to her parents and fiancé. Women, she explained to her brother, were "like Clay in the Hands of the Artist." Her artist got his way; by May a summer wedding was being planned. Only the clergy of the Church of England could perform marriages. The Archbishop of Canterbury graciously granted a special license for a ceremony outside a church, but the parents wanted no ordinary Anglican priest to officiate. They prevailed upon Jonathan Shipley, the only bishop to support the colonies throughout the Revolution, to do so. Since he was leaving town for the summer, Nabby and William were quickly and privately married in June, only ten months after she had broken her engagement to Tyler.

Her daughter's wedding agitated Abigail as much as her own, twenty-two years before. The night before she dreamed of Tyler, and the night after she could not sleep. Well pleased with her son-in-law, she still felt guilty in giving the passive Nabby to any man. Had this only daughter grown up with sisters, she might have turned out more spirited: this thought was as far as Abigail went in admitting failure to prepare Nabby to make the most of the female role. The realization that her daughter was in fact married and no longer under her protection came home to Abigail for the first time at the beginning of July, when the newlyweds moved into their own house. Though the Smiths were only a half mile away and dined daily in the legation, she more than ever felt alone.

Thomas Jefferson in Paris remained a source of strength and joy to the Adamses during their London years. The Virginian corresponded with the interesting Mrs. Adams, whose company he had enjoyed and whose management of her husband's pecuniary affairs he had observed with admiration. Their letters provide evidence of an intellectual exchange, not the least patronizing on his part, of a similar republican outlook on monarchial and aristocratic European society, and of a closeness in small ways that denoted kindred spirits. They exchanged favors: she shopped in London for his shirts and table linen; he sent her shoes, dress materials, and decorative tableware. In the spring of 1786, when Jefferson spent several weeks in London on diplomatic business, they personally renewed their friendship.

The following year Abigail became involved briefly in one of the most controversial chapters of Jefferson's life. When his younger daughter passed through England on the way to France, he requested Abigail to care for the eight-year-old. A very frightened "Polly" (Maria) Jefferson reached London in June 1787, but a few days of loving care by the Adamses calmed her fears and won her trust. Then in two weeks Abigail had to force the sobbing girl into the carriage of the French-speaking servant her father had sent for her.

The old nurse who had been expected to accompany Polly became ill and had been replaced by Sally Hemings, a light-skinned, pretty slave of fourteen, daughter of Jefferson's father-in-law by a mulatto concubine. From Sally's physical development, Abigail judged her to be older, but after a few days concluded that she was "quite a child" and "wholy incapable of looking properly after" Polly. Letters to Jefferson emphasized this judgment as a way of registering an opinion that Sally should be sent home, for Abigail well understood the temptation this attractive girl would offer a widower of Jefferson's sensibility.

Nevertheless, Sally went off to Paris, dressed in the calico Abigail had purchased for her while shopping for finer clothes for Polly. She remained during Jefferson's stay in France and returned to Virginia with him in 1789. Stories of "Dusky Sally," whose offspring at Monticello were reported to resemble closely their master, would be broadcast by Federalist Party mudslingers in the campaign of 1800, and modern biographers still debate the relationship of Jefferson to his slave woman. Had he heeded Abigail's advice, there would have been no grounds for suspicion.

Abigail displayed a growing concern that her countrymen lacked the virtue needed to sustain their new republic. She was reminded of America's libertarian heritage in July 1786 when the family visited the country estate of Thomas Brand Hollis, heir to the philanthropist Thomas Hollis, who in the decades before the Revolution had given the library of Harvard College most of its books on government: the very volumes from which students like John Adams had imbibed their ideas on freedom. That same summer she accompanied her husband to Holland on a diplomatic errand. In this small republic, where she was treated as a lady of distinction, she learned a political lesson by watching the Utrecht Patriots, a party of solid middle-class burghers, strengthen their constitution against the forces of hereditary aristocracy, only later to have this reform overturned by Prussian troops backed by British gold.

In the last days of 1786 Abigail had another close look at the corrupting influences she hoped Americans could avoid, when she and the Smiths visited the famous resort town of Bath. A week of balls, concerts, plays, private parties, and walks and meals in fashionable places left her thoroughly satiated. She described Bath as "one constant Scene of dissipation and Gambling from Monday morning till Saturday Night." On the trip back to London her mind was occupied in "a train of moral reflections," during which she considered anew the first question of the catechism on which generations of New England children had been raised: "What is the Chief end of Man?"

Abigail took comfort from the thought that her sons were being educated far from the moral cesspools of Europe. Yet she and John were abandoning the hope that the American Revolution had given birth to a citizenry with the will to spurn the political and social degeneracy of the Old World. Americans were spending millions for English luxury goods at a time when the United States could not fund its foreign and domestic debts and thus establish its credit abroad. "Luxery always leads to Idleness, Indolence and effeminancy," she lectured Johnny. Witness, for example, the American states that now for selfish reasons withheld "from Congress those powers which would enable" it to "give vigor and strength" to its proceedings and at times even failed to send the delegates necessary to make the quorum required to conduct the nation's business.

John had soon realized that the weakness of the American government under the Articles of Confederation rendered futile his negotiations with the British. Congress could not prevent the states from violating the peace treaty of 1783 by restricting the return of loyalists and placing obstacles in the path of English merchants seeking to collect pre-Revolutionary debts. The British used these violations as a justification for continuing to occupy several forts in the Northwest Territory of the United States and for refusing to pay for slaves taken off during the late war. Furthermore, Great Britain had nothing to gain and much to lose by readmitting American ships to their most lucrative prewar markets in the British empire.

When reports reached the Adamses of the revolt in western Massachusetts of debtors led by Captain Daniel Shays, Abigail cried over the disgrace of her country. She could not hold back the tears at the thought of her "Countrymen who had so nobly fought and bled for freedom, tarnishing their glory, loosing the bonds of society, introducing anarchy confusion and despotism, forging domestick Chains for posterity."

The "experience of ages, and the Historick page" had taught her that popular tyranny invariably led to the "arbitrary government of a Single person."

John's answer to Shays's Rebellion, to the weakness of the Confederation government, and to European criticism of the American state constitutions was feverish work on the three volumes of *A Defence of the Constitutions of Government in the United States of America.* With this treatise he hoped to supply a practical manual for preserving and strengthening republican governments. As Mr. Adams rethought his political philosophy in the direction of checks on licentious political behavior, Mrs. Adams denounced to Jefferson the Massachusetts rebels as "Ignorant, wrestless, desperadoes, [who] without conscience or principals, have led a deluded multitude to follow their standard, under pretence of grievences which have no existance but in their immaginations." Jefferson's reply suggested the coming divergence of their political views: "The spirit of resistance to government is so valuable on certain occasions, that I wish it always kept alive. It will often be exercised when wrong, but better so than not to be exercised at all. I like a little rebellion now and then." Yielding not an inch, Abigail answered that an unprincipled mob was the "worst of all Tyrannies."

Reports that Hancock had declined reelection and that their friend Governor James Bowdoin was vigorously suppressing the rebellion heartened the Adamses. They took hope too from news of a convention in Philadelphia to revise the Articles of Confederation. Their years in Europe had weaned them from a primary allegiance to their state; now they believed that a stable political order required a strong central government with power to coerce the states on vital national concerns. At John's direction, Abigail instructed Cotton Tufts to invest small sums in the badly depreciated securities of Congress. They already held "Congress paper" and Masssachusetts loan certificates; so, she reasoned, "if one Sinks all must Sink, which God forbid."

By the summer of 1787 Abigail longed for home. During May and June, John left her to go to Amsterdam to complete still another loan from Dutch bankers. Nothing made her more homesick than missing the Harvard Commencement in July, where Johnny took his degree and distinguished himself as a class orator. Abigail's health had been poorer the past year. For three weeks she lay ill and had to be bled to relieve a "swimming" in the head. She was overjoyed that Nabby had given birth to a healthy son; but being a grandmother caused Abigail to think, as she neared forty-three, that she was entering a period of life when friends and neighbors at home would be especially dear. Then by fall Braintree held a new appeal. Cotton Tufts wrote that he had been able to buy the Vassall-Borland estate for them. This was the fine home, by Braintree standards, that Royall Tyler had let go when his engagement to Nabby had crumbled. After living in two European mansions, Mrs. Adams hoped to return to a dwelling more appropriate to the rank of a retired ambassador than their humble cottage. By November she was issuing instructions to Uncle Tufts for refurbishing her new house.

Congress granted John's request to return. While he wound up his official business, Abigail supervised the packing and said a heart-rending farewell to the Smiths, who sailed to New York on another ship. Only separation from her daughter for the first time made Abigail regret leaving England. The condition of Esther, the American maid, complicated the return. After appearing seriously ill for months before even the physician suspected her pregnancy, Esther hastily married the father, John Briesler, the other American servant. But Abigail dreaded the prospect of being midwife for a shipboard delivery. On April 20, 1788, the Adams party boarded the *Lucretia* to sail for Boston.

Their three years in London had strengthened the bonds between Abigail and John. She had so merged her ambition with his that she functioned as a true alter ego. The feeling of being alone together in a hostile country had strengthened their love and companionship, and John's lack of diplomatic success had left time for pleasant holidays together. There remained, even after almost a quarter century, enough sensuality in their marriage to motivate a little sexual teasing by mail when they were apart. Rather than a treaty with Great Britain, they brought home greater love and respect for each other.

During the voyage Abigail reflected on her European experience. She had "seen enough of the world" and would hereafter be content to learn what was "further to be known from the page of History." Her four years abroad had not been the most pleasant part of her life, for she preferred the "Domestick happiness and Rural felicity" of Braintree. Yet she did not regret the European excursion, for it had strengthened her attachment to America.

Fearful for her country's future, she nevertheless considered it a near paradise as compared with England, that "boasted Island of Liberty," where freedom meant only the liberty of the upper classes to oppress the poor. When she reflected upon "the advantages which the people of

America possess, over the most polish'd of other Nations, the ease with which property is obtain'd, the plenty which is so equally distributed, the personal Liberty, and Security of Life and property," she gave thanks to heaven for having cast her "Lot in that happy land."

VIII

"In Their Proper Sphere"

1788–1792

Abigail Adams summoned all her courage and patience to endure the slow return voyage during the stormiest spring the sailors could recall. At the end of May she wrote, "I hope and pray, I may never again be left to go to sea: of all places it is the most disagreeable." Her spirits rose when she successfully assisted in the birth of Esther's daughter on the high seas. Then the reception they received upon landing at Boston on June 17, 1788, drove the frightful voyage from her mind.

John Adams came home to a hero's welcome. The cannon of the harbor fort saluted the ship's approach. Thousands of citizens cheered him at dockside. He and his wife rode in state to the governor's mansion, and Boston's church bells pealed until sundown, while the town's dignitaries called to offer greetings. This hero's welcome acknowledged that Adams, alone of the original Massachusetts Revolutionary leaders, had put on the mantle of a national statesman in the postwar period. Yet their homecoming had a bittersweet taste because Abigail and John knew that the elaborate reception had been carefully orchestrated by John Hancock, a master at such public spectacles. The crisis of Shays's Rebellion past, Hancock had ended his brief political retirement and been easily reelected governor. Now there were rumors that he expected the presidency, or at least the vice presidency, a prospect at which the Adamses shuddered. They proceeded as quietly as possible to Braintree for a joyous reunion with their boys and a host of relatives and friends.

After four years in European mansions, Mrs. Adams felt keen disappointment as she inspected her new home. Much smaller than she remembered, she had the feeling of being in a "wren's house." The low ceilings, empty rooms, and general disrepair made it seem more like a barracks than a home. "The Garden was a wilderness" and the property lacked every essential for farming. John and Abigail gave the whole summer to making the house livable and redeeming the fields from years of neglect. The furniture and china brought back from Europe, though somewhat damaged in shipment, lent an air of luxury. By September Abigail was ready to entertain Hancock and the officers of a French fleet then in port. A niece, unacquainted with European courts, dined with them and afterwards noted in her diary that "we had a very elegant dinner."

Though worried over his future, John Adams enjoyed these months spent as a gentleman farmer. He busied himself directing the workmen—as many as ten at once—whom he employed to build stone walls, dig ditches, clear the fields, and repair the house. Abigail disliked all this commotion and fretted over John's expenditures. Still, the joy of being reunited with her sons and sister made her feel at home in this strange house. She was now so close to the Cranches that the two families could visit almost daily, and other nearby relatives often joined them.

Yet separation from Nabby left a large void in Abigail's life, and even more so when she learned that her daughter was pregnant again and surrounded by dominating in-laws near New York City. Nabby soon adjusted to her new surroundings with typical acquiescence and kept her parents informed of the political climate of New York. In November Abigail traveled south to be present at the birth, but the baby—John Adams

Smith—arrived before she did. After six weeks in New York, she made the two-hundred-mile homeward journey in a sleigh, bringing Nabby, Colonel Smith, and the new grandson for a visit.

Abigail had gone to New York at the time the states that had ratified the Constitution were beginning to consider their choices for President and Vice President. John would not budge from his farm for fear he would be accused of office-seeking. Abigail promised him that she would be politically discreet during her trip, that she would "hear all" but "say little." She soon discovered that her husband's future was the subject of widespread speculation, even in the inns along the road. Once she reached the Smith estate, John Jay drove out for a serious talk. Though he had also been mentioned for the vice presidency, Jay expressed a strong desire to see his former diplomatic colleague in a national office. Then Colonel Smith brought word back from his club, of which Alexander Hamilton, the self-appointed kingmaker, was a member, that Virginia would join Hamilton's friends in supporting Adams for the second position. Before going home, Abigail spent several days in New York as the house guest of the Jays, where she was besieged by important visitors wanting to make her acquaintance. Her journey served a political purpose, even if neither she nor John would admit the possibility.

Knowing that he could not compete with Washington for the presidency, John Adams craved the office next in rank, to which he believed his services entitled him. But even more he saw the coming election as a test of whether strong, independent men would fill the executive branch established by the Constitution. In Abigail's words, he was a man who "will never hide or conceal a Sentiment of his Heart from the people which he thinks [it is] for their interest or happiness to be acquainted with, tho he should forfeit by it the highest offices in the United States." He had broadcast his political sentiments widely in the *Defence of the Constitutions*. Abandoning his earlier hope that the Revolution had given birth to a nation of virtuous citizens, he concluded that postwar Americans had shown all those human passions that led inevitably to distinctions of wealth and rank in every society. The unavoidable clash between aristocracy and democracy, even in republican America, would destroy free government unless a strong and independent executive preserved the balance. By the time he returned to his homeland, some critics called him a monarchist and others lamented that this honest diplomat had lost touch with his democratic countrymen. Now he remained in Braintree, thinking himself too honest to be popular. While refusing all lesser offices, he determined not to lift a finger to solicit the position he deserved.

Abigail's encouraging news from New York lifted her husband's spirits. By the first of March he knew he would be chosen Vice President, but he was crushed when the final electoral vote arrived. According to the Constitution, each of the sixty-nine electors cast two votes, the candidate receiving a majority to be President and the second highest, Vice President. Washington's vote was unanimous, while Adams had only thirty-four. After considerable agonizing he convinced himself that the salvation of the country required him to accept this humiliating elevation to national office. He did not know that Hamilton had campaigned to get him out of the way by raising him to the impotent office of Vice President with a vote sufficiently low to dim his political future. There was some consolation in Hancock's receiving only four votes; and as Adams traveled alone to New York in April to assume his duties, the towns along the way greeted him so enthusiastically that his bruised pride was considerably healed. His popularity in New England had never been greater.

Abigail believed that John's sacrifices for his country entitled him to its highest offices; had he practiced law instead of statesmanship the family would have been wealthy. She saw herself as an equal sufferer in these losses; indeed, she insisted that she had sacrificed more "than any other woman in the Country." (She apparently meant more than any wife of the leaders, not the thousands of poor women, white and black, now often widows.) Consequently, she expected to reap an equal share of whatever honor and preferment her husband might receive from a country ungrateful in the past. At the same time, she worried that she might unconsciously put on airs that would offend her intimate friends and requested her sister to watch for such signs.

Abigail's political philosophy mirrored John's. Yet her eclectic reading and insightful observations of men and manners enabled her to illustrate and apply his political thought with force and clarity. Like him, she no longer believed that the masses could become enlightened or that American republicanism could bring about a universal moral revival. All people throughout history displayed the same fundamental needs and were driven by the same passions. She observed to her daughter, "I am sometimes led to think that humane nature is a very perverse thing, and much more given to evil than good." To preserve American freedom, enlightened and virtuous leaders had to preside over the government. Ideally, though, an elite of virtue and wisdom, not of wealth or heredity, should govern.

As a result, for Abigail and John every national election was a test of whether free government could survive or whether the United States would turn toward monarchy and aristocracy to preserve social order.

The Adamses therefore subjected all men in public life to the most rigorous scrutiny and were quick to attribute to others the shortcomings they feared in themselves. They now regarded their former close friend James Warren as an insincere patriot for repeatedly refusing to abandon the comfort of home for public service and for favoring Shays's Rebellion. And they considered Mercy Otis Warren a poor example of republican womanhood, since she had been unwilling to give up her husband to the state for long periods. Abigail and John may have been unusually censorious, but the standards of political virtue they advocated for others they applied to themselves. His contemporaries described John Adams as vain, stubborn, pedantic, and irritable, but often in the same breath acknowledged his incorruptible integrity and independence of judgment. When Abigail held John up as a paragon of political virtue, she was not entirely deceived by her love for him.

In following her husband's changing political thought, Abigail revealed the limits of her advocacy of the emancipation of women. She now re-

garded females in general to be no more capable
of enlightenment than males. Consequently, no
mass reformation of American women would
preserve the republic. The hope lay rather in at-
taching equal importance to the education of the
sexes so that both might "move with honour and
dignity in their proper Sphere." The proper
sphere for women was marriage and motherhood, and conjugal fidelity stood highest in the
"Ranks of Female virtues." The future of the
country depended on creating homes where loving, educated, devout parents brought up boys
qualified for republican leadership and girls of
sufficient virtue to be wives and mothers to patriots. Abigail worried lest American women, unacquainted with "the more than Egyptian Bondage,
to which the Female Sex, have been subjugated
from the earliest ages," fail to profit from their
relatively favorable situation in the United States.
"The free and confidential intercourse between
the Sexes is no where to be found with equal Security and purity as in this Country, ... conce-
quently there is more conjugal Fidelity and domestic happiness here than is to be found any
where else." American women should prove
themselves worthy of the freedom they already
enjoyed before demanding more.

Abigail gently taunted John with the judgment
of historians that those few queens who had

ruled as absolute monarchs had generally been good sovereigns. She wanted republican women also to be good sovereigns, but in emulation of her own example. As she once declared to John, "my ambition will extend no further than Reigning in the Heart of my Husband. That is my Throne and there I aspire to be absolute." For her, then, any further emancipation of American women must take place within the confines of marriage, rational Christianity, and republican institutions. Women must be as zealous to preserve what they had already attained as to work for new gains. The daughters and granddaughters of the American Revolution had more to fear from social revolutionaries than from the tyranny of husbands. The position she had reached by 1790 was clear: "Tho' as females we have no voice in Legislation, yet is our happiness so blended and interwoven with those who have, that we have every reason to rejoice in the improvement of science and the advancement of civilization which has proved so favorable to our sex, and has lead mankind to consider us in a much more respectable light than we deserve."

Like Judith Sargent Murray, the gifted Massachusetts woman who in 1790 published a magazine essay "On the Equality of the Sexes," Abigail was encouraged by the establishment of schools and other evidence of an increased concern for female education since the Revolution. More had been done, she observed, "within these last 15 Years than for a whole Century before." She also took heart from the work of Mary Wollstonecraft, whose *A Vindication of the Rights of Women* had editions in Boston and Philadelphia the same year (1792) it was published in London. Abigail disliked the radical political views of Wollstonecraft's earlier book on the French Revolution and must have been disturbed by her attack on James Fordyce as a betrayer of women.

Nonetheless, Abigail appreciated the attention this outspoken English woman had called to the debasement of females and to the masculine scorn of feminine characteristics. In 1794 John teasingly addressed his wife as a "Disciple of Woolstoncraft." In return she advised him to become a "pupil" of Wollstonecraft and "confess the Truth, and own that when you are sick of the Ambition, the intrigues, the duplicity and the Treachery of the aspiring part of your own Sex, it is a comfort and a consolation to retire to the Simplicity, the Gentleness and tenderness of the Female Character."

Abigail remained closer to Fordyce than to Wollstonecraft. She steadfastly held to the view that education remained the best hope for the advancement of women. But she also feared that the present direction of American society would weaken those values to which she attributed the relative emancipation of women in the United States as compared with their European sisters. Virtuous and educated republican mothers therefore had to give a large share of their time to training their children for moral and political leadership. They should "always keep in mind the great importance of first principles, and the necessity of instilling the precepts of morality very early into their minds." Children's literature should teach "brotherly love, sisterly affection, and filial respect and reverence." And it was necessary to keep the children of such mothers from mixing with servants and others who did not hold proper standards of virtue. The more conservative her political philosophy became, the more Abigail laid the responsibility for the republic's future at the feet of American mothers.

John Adams was a vigorous fifty-three when he became Vice President. Except for weak eyes and occasional tremors of the hands, his health had never been better. Nine years younger, Abigail Adams had suffered a lifetime of erratic health. Fevers, nervous disorders, and rheumatic pains plagued her seasonally. She knew that menopause was approaching and dreaded its effects. Still, chronic illness had seldom prevented her from carrying out her duties. During the next twelve years, however, her health had an increasing influence on John's career and at times on the nation's business. But in the meantime she was to spend one of her happiest years while the federal government resided in New York City.

After learning of his election, Vice President Adams left hurriedly for New York, once again dumping their domestic affairs in his wife's lap. In May he rented a house and wrote Abigail to come. She took a month to make arrangements for the farm, to select the furniture to be crated and shipped, and to pack personal effects. Charles would miss his Harvard Commencement to live with his parents. Since his reputation for keeping bad company in college already greatly troubled his mother, she hoped that the father's influence would prove remedial, despite even greater temptations in the metropolitan environment of New York City. Tommy would remain at college and John Quincy with his law studies in Newburyport, Massachusetts. To Abigail's delight, John had already given Nabby and her family permission to move into the house.

A difficult journey by road and coastal packet brought Abigail's party to New York in June. Once she laid eyes on her new home at Richmond Hill, she quickly forgot the rigors of travel. From the beginning she delighted in this spacious house situated on a hill overlooking the

Hudson River and surrounded by greenery. Best of all, Nabby was there to embrace her mother.

The next morning Abigail took her daughter and hastened to call on Martha Washington. She knew well the necessity of establishing a friendship with the First Lady. During his days in the Continental Congress John's suspicion of military power had won him a reputation of hostility toward the commander-in-chief. James Madison, for one, had suggested that the Vice President might become an active rival of the President. The Adamses resolved to quiet such rumors by every possible means.

It turned out to be an easy task, for genuine respect and affection developed between the two families. The wives felt an instant attraction to each other. Abigail admired the President's "grace, dignity and ease," qualities in which she judged him vastly superior to George III. Whenever the Vice President's wife entered Mrs. Washington's drawing room, the President at once cleared a place for her at the right of his wife. While in New York, the families were together frequently, as often in private as at public affairs. Though never able to suppress entirely his jealousy of the Virginian, John agreed with Abigail's "firm opinion" that Washington was the hope of the country, that "no other man could rule over this great people and consolidate them into one mighty Empire but He who is set over us." She trembled at the thought that he might die in office before the government under the Constitution was securely established and leave John to wrestle with difficulties that could "carry him perhaps to an early Grave with misery and disgrace." His emphasis on the necessity of a powerful executive led John to push unsuccessfully to have the President addressed by a title such as "His Most Benign Highness," and once in a letter to her sister Abigail referred to him as "His Majesty." Still, John's inveterate wariness kept him at more distance from the great man than Abigail would have liked.

John had soon realized that his office bore no responsibility except the tedious daily task of presiding over the Senate, where he had a vote only in case of a tie. It became apparent also that Washington consulted him only rarely on major decisions. The office was further demeaned when Congress voted the President a salary of $25,000 a year but gave the Vice President only $5,000. Grumbling as he did over his insignificant position, John carried out his duties religiously. In an evenly divided Senate, he broke several ties on crucial issues in favor of the administration. Abigail insisted on the importance of her husband's contribution in words such as she wrote to Mary Cranch: "If the United States had chosen to the Vice P's Chair a man wavering in his opinions, or one who sought the popular applause of the multitude, this very constitution would have had its death wound during the first six months of its existance."

As a whole, the organization of the new government much pleased the Adamses. Their friend Jay received his preferred appointment as Chief Justice of the Supreme Court. Jefferson came back from France to become Secretary of State and to renew their friendship in person. With these two in office, Abigail considered the outlook for the republic favorable, provided that restless agitators be not "permitted to sow the seeds of discord among the real defenders of the faith." Among these "real defenders" she included Hamilton, whose financial measures—"the Great National System"—she endorsed enthusiastically. Her son Charles was indeed fortunate, she believed, to have had the privilege of studying law with Hamilton for a few months before that brilliant young statesman assumed his cabinet position. Madison's growing opposition to Hamilton's proposals, in Abigail's eyes, constituted evidence that the "Father of the Constitution" was at best learned rather than wise, and at worst had "designs" contrary to the country's welfare.

Even on the limited salary granted the Vice President, Abigail ran a household of eighteen and entertained freely. She scoffed at reports in the newspapers that the high officers of the government wallowed in luxury and dissipation. It was true that several ladies held regular evenings at home—among them Mrs. Adams on Fridays and Mrs. Washington on Mondays—so that one could go visiting five nights a week, but only for a few minutes of conversation spiced with tea, coffee, lemonade, and perhaps cake. The President's levees went so far as to serve ice cream in the summer, an indulgence hardly likely to destroy the moral fiber of the republic. After witnessing the extravagance of European courts, Abigail saw no need to apologize for modest dinners or for accepting the President's invitation to sit in his box at the theater. Still, her happy year in the first federal capital city was best for those hours spent with Nabby, grandchildren, and a few close friends. Only the Sundays marred her happiness, for nearly all the non-Anglican ministers of New York were disciples of "good old Calvin" and ranted self-righteously in support of the rigid theology incompatible with her rational faith.

On July 10, 1790, Abigail surely felt considerable satisfaction with the new nation her husband had helped to create. That Saturday President Washington led the Vice President, the secretaries of State, Treasury, and War, together with their wives and some members of their families, on an inspection of Fort Washington, site of a disastrous American defeat in the War for Independence. Afterwards, in an act of symbolic triumph, the party sat down to dinner in a mansion formerly belonging to a loyalist. As she dined on this pleasant day with Jefferson and Hamilton, Abigail knew that they had struck a bargain to move the federal government to Philadelphia for ten years and then to a permanent site on the Potomac River.

For weeks she had been tormented with the "apprehension of a Removal from a very delightfull situation." Now that the question was settled, she wrote John Quincy that "it will be a grevious thing to me to be obliged to leave this delicious Spot, your Sister and the children, your Brother and other connection[s], Yet for the sake of peace, harmony and justice I am Submissive." At the end of August she said a "most tender and affectionate" farewell to Mrs. Washington, who was returning to Mount Vernon. In September John rode to Philadelphia, rented a house, and came back to move his family.

Abigail's mind was preoccupied with her children as she watched the much-traveled furniture once again being crated. Tommy, fresh from his Harvard Commencement, had arrived in New York to accompany his parents to Philadelphia, where he planned to study law. This choice of a vocation pleased the father, but his mother had reservations: "I wish he could have gone into merchandize as I am sure he has more of a Turn for active Life." Yet she took comfort in having at least one child with her in their new home. There was no moving Charles from New York, for he hoped in time to open a law office in this growing metropolis. He would live with the Smiths, who had already gone to housekeeping for themselves, but for the first time since his graduation he would be out from under the parental scrutiny that had kept him from loose companions.

With John Quincy, now in his mid-twenties, Abigail had a different concern. Admitted to the Massachusetts bar, he waited impatiently in Boston for clients. Meanwhile he had experienced a belated awakening to the opposite sex. At the moment he was completely taken with Mary Frazier of Newburyport. Still dependent on his parents for partial support, the young lawyer was in no position to take a wife. He knew it, his mother knew it, and she drove the point home in several loving but firm letters. "A too early Marriage," she wrote, "will involve you in troubles that may render you and yours unhappy the remainder of your Life." It was unfair to any woman, she added, to win her affections with no prospect of supporting her adequately in marriage. Half seriously, Abigail did see one benefit from Johnny's love affair: it might correct his sloppiness of dress and person. He replied with dutiful assurances that he had put aside for the time being all thoughts of a connection with any woman. There were obvious signs, however, that this continued repression of his sexual drive troubled him deeply.

As an object lesson, Abigail pressed upon Johnny the plight of his sister. Colonel Smith had found no profitable employment since returning from England. Instead of taking his father-in-law's advice to go into law, he sought government service. His present position as federal marshal paid not nearly enough to support his expensive habits and growing family. Nabby had just given birth to a third son. "Heaven grant," implored her mother, "that she may add no more to the Stock untill her prospects brighten." The colonel then sailed with little notice for England to sell American lands and securities and to act as confidential agent for Hamilton's pro-British party. He left his wife with a seriously ill baby and left his in-laws—who did not fully know the purpose of his trip—disillusioned with their daughter's marriage.

An "intermitting" fever made Abigail's last month in New York miserable, but she improved somewhat during the five-day trip to Philadelphia, where they arrived in mid-November. The first weeks were spent in making the house at Bush Hill habitable and caring for several members of the household taken sick. Tommy had such acute rheumatism that "after having been 9 times Bled, puked and many other applications," he still could not walk or feed himself. As Tommy gradually improved, so did Abigail's spirits, most of all when Johnny and Charles arrived for a long winter visit.

Social life in Philadelphia was even more extensive than in New York. Calls, theater, teas, balls, parties, and receptions could fill six evenings a week and as many afternoons. Abigail drew the line, though, at Saturday evening affairs. Her optimism for the new government soared in the winter of 1790–1791. All states had ratified the Constitution. American securities sold in Amsterdam at par or above. "Our publick affairs never looked more prosperous," she informed her sister. Among the good news was the appointment of Colonel Smith to be supervisor of the federal excise for the State of New York, a position offering a modest but steady income. Her mind relieved of a very heavy burden, his mother-in-law urged him to come home and get to work.

After Congress adjourned, Abigail and John set out for Braintree early in May, with a stop in New York to see Nabby. There Abigail was taken ill and suffered throughout the remainder of the trip. The ague, a recurrent malarial fever, left her too weak to walk unassisted at the end of their journey. She spent a quiet summer recuperating. Nabby came for a visit, while her husband, back from Europe, vainly attempted to secure the nomination as minister to Great Britain. He had no chance, for Jefferson knew that the colonel was being used by Hamilton in an effort to undermine the Secretary of State's foreign policy.

In October the Adamses returned to Philadelphia. This time they insisted on having a residence in the center of the town to avoid daily commuting to Bush Hill in the suburbs. They had to take a smaller house at a higher price, or, according to John, a democratic house at a princely rent. Being in the city brought more company to their door, notwithstanding their reduced facilities for entertaining. After several weeks of better health and much socializing, Abigail was laid low with "Inflamitory Rhumatism" followed by a return of the ague. Unable to leave her chamber for six weeks, she was bled three times and had eight pairs of blisters applied to her wrists. She possessed a great faith in the common medical practice of bloodletting to relieve the flushed appearance of a feverish patient, and she believed in the curative power of blistering agents to purge the body of poisons.

An irritant, commonly the Spanish fly, applied to tender areas, raised first- or second-degree burns which became infected and excreted pus, the supposed poison.

By the time Congress adjourned late in April 1792, she was still emaciated and weak but would not hear of spending the summer in Philadelphia's unhealthy climate. They traveled slowly northward, stopping in New York to see Charles. This visit depressed Abigail's spirits further, for Nabby and her grandsons were not there. Colonel Smith had sailed with them to England a month before on another speculative venture. Nabby had considered her husband's prospects encouraging and attempted to reassure her parents. But in view of Abigail's health and the recent death of Nabby's baby boy, it had been a sad separation for both mother and daughter.

The Adamses returned not to Braintree but to Quincy. In February the North Precinct of Braintree had been incorporated as a separate town named for John Quincy, Abigail's grandfather. The Vice President and his wife were saved much embarrassment when the town meeting narrowly defeated a proposal to name the new town after another famous man born there, John Hancock. Relations between these close friends of Revolutionary days had become openly strained. John thought that most people now realized that Hancock was a "mere rich Man privileged of his Wealth to obtain an empty Bubble of Popularity." Moreover, he considered that the senile Samuel Adams had dishonored himself by fawning over Hancock to gain office as lieutenant governor.

After a summer at home, Abigail still did not think herself well enough to undertake the three-hundred-mile journey to Philadelphia and risk a winter in its damp air. John would go alone to preside over the Senate and await the results of the 1792 presidential election. When he left Abigail late in November, she experienced again that deep loneliness she had known when her husband first went to Europe. But now for the first time since her marriage none of the immediate family lived with her.

Nearing her forty-eighth birthday, Abigail acknowledged that she had entered menopause, a "critical period of Life [that] Augments my complaints." With her last pregnancy fifteen years behind her, she did not welcome this physical change as a respite from childbearing. She believed bleeding necessary to ease the symptoms of menopause, thus placing it in the category of illness. In this state of mind, not for five years would she feel able to rejoin her husband in the nation's capital.

Nevertheless, the tenderness between them grew. Defections from virtue, honor, and wisdom in their former friends—Hancock, Samuel Adams, the Warrens, and soon Jefferson—drew this husband and wife together. A month after he left for Philadelphia, John wrote, "I am as impatient to see you as I used to be twenty years ago." She replied: "Years subdue the ardour of passion but in lieu thereof a Friendship and affection deep rooted subsists which defies the Ravages of Time, and will survive whilst the vital Flame exists. Our attachment to Character, Reputation and Fame increase I believe with our Years."

IX

"Tellegraph
of the Mind"

1792–1797

The French Revolution increased the concern of the Adamses over the direction of American society. John saw the radical course of events in France as proof of the political theories advanced in his books. Abigail displayed more anxiety over the social and moral implications for the United States of the French experience. Until now her eclectic mind had drawn from eighteenth-century thought whatever she found stimulating or satisfying, with little concern for religious orthodoxy. She had been as much at home with the freethinker Jefferson and the liberal Richard Price as with the moderate Calvinist Samuel Cooper, and much more so than with rigid Calvinistic or evangelical preachers. The attempt of the French revolutionaries to eradicate Christianity impressed upon her for the first time the dangerous tendency of liberal religion to drift into deism and atheism and in so doing to destroy the essential foundation of society.

In disgust at the preachers she heard in New York, Abigail exclaimed in 1790, "O when when shall I hear the Candour and liberal good sense of a Price again, animated with true piety without enthusiasm, devotion without grimace and Religion upon a Rational system." By then, her favorite preacher had become a storm center in Europe as the result of his widely published sermon praising the French Revolution and calling for reforms in England. Price sent the Adamses a copy, to which John replied with only restrained approval. Unlike Price, he saw a wide difference between the American and French revolutions, for France, a nation of "thirty million atheists," had undertaken its revolution to achieve the impossible goal of "equality of persons and property." Abigail was saddened to read that Price went to his grave in 1791 before realizing the errors into which zeal for liberty had led him. She had learned from his example that liberal religion might blind one to the reality of the human condition.

Abigail possessed a deep and intense religious faith. In earlier years it had been largely a personal faith on which she had relied during births, illnesses, deaths, and long absences from her husband. Now in full maturity she had concluded that the neglect of religion lay at the heart of most social and political problems, because true religion was "the only Sure and certain Security, which binds man to Man and renders him responsible to his Maker." Dislike of the metaphysical subtleties of Calvinists or Trinitarians did not lessen her insistence that Christianity continue to be the foundation of American republican society. "I am no friend of bigotry," she wrote Nabby; "yet I think the freedom of inquiry, and the general toleration of religious sentiments, have been, like all other good things, perverted, and, under that shelter, deism, and even atheism, have found refuge." Americans had to preserve their belief in the God of the Bible, in the afterlife as the only truly happy existence, in God-given responsibilities in this world as the means of achieving happiness in the next, and in "the over ruling hand of providence fulfilling great designs" in human history. Life was essentially tragic, and whatever limited progress mankind achieved resulted from the development of individual virtue, not from revolution. The great fountain of virtue for her remained the teaching of enlightened but devout Christianity. Abigail and John shared this faith;

but religion for him was philosophical and academic, while for her it was pragmatic and personal. Here, as in other ways, this wife and husband nicely balanced each other. For her part she taught John that religious faith must be emotionally as well as intellectually satisfying.

Abigail sensed from her close association with Thomas Jefferson in France that he was deficient in religion. In practice the Massachusetts housewife and the Virginia planter exemplified many of the same fundamental values, but in theory he advocated a natural religion that had no place for the supernatural verities to which she clung. To this deficiency of belief she in part attributed his political errors of the 1790s. The gradual alienation between Jefferson and the Adamses was both a national and a personal tragedy. Gentleman farmer John Adams was closer in spirit and practice to planter Thomas Jefferson than to financier Alexander Hamilton. Abigail and John passionately defended the Secretary of the Treasury's plan to secure the credit of the United States, but they had no enthusiasm for his federally chartered bank and the financial community forming around it. As they learned more of Hamilton's electioneering jobbery, they lost faith in popular elections. Hamilton shrewdly understood that an Adams-Jefferson coalition would be his undoing and had worked to prevent it. Had such a coalition developed, the Virginian would have tempered Adams's fear of popular sovereignty, and the Yankee would have taught Jefferson something of the contradictions in his democratic philosophy. They needed each other and the country needed them together.

Abigail still valued her past friendship with Jefferson, but she now called to mind other signs of moral weakness in the slave owner and the widower who had never remarried. And John reminded Abigail that he believed Jefferson still owed large debts to English merchants, with the implication that herein lay the reason for his partiality to France. There was no shortage of explanations for his fall from virtue, and Abigail and John confirmed each other's suspicions that he had fallen.

This alienation from their dear friend made transparent the one detrimental aspect of their remarkable marital relationship. Such closeness, such love and respect for each other fused two minds into one. As Abigail explained, "our Thoughts run in the same channel. . . . [It] may be call'd the Tellegraph of the Mind." She almost always accepted her husband's lead in political philosophy and practical politics. She admitted as much by quoting to him the words of an English writer: "I have a good opinion of my politics, since they agree with a Man who always thinks so justly." Consequently, she energetically confirmed, intensified, and defended but almost never took issue with his public positions. Given the personality of John Adams, his wife's talents contributed somewhat to his failure to develop a larger measure of those political skills necessary for effective leadership in a republic with democratic impulses.

In typical fashion, John had reacted to the French Revolution by writing a long series of anonymous newspaper essays in 1790 and 1791. The "Discourses on Davila" defended his view that political freedom could be preserved only by a balanced government effectively controlling the natural rivalry of men for wealth and distinction. Inevitably, then, the quest of the French for equality would bring chaos and the eventual loss of the freedom they sought. Along with many Americans, Jefferson viewed events in France as a praiseworthy effort to follow the American example of 1776. In a private letter to a Philadelphia printer, he endorsed *The Rights of Man,* Thomas Paine's eloquent answer to critics of the French revolutionaries. The printer, without Jefferson's knowledge, included this letter in the foreword of a new edition. Since the letter contained a veiled reference to the "political heresies" of Adams's "Discourses on Davila," the Secretary of State appeared to be taking public issue with the Vice President. Eager to defend his father, John Quincy rejected Paine's argument for the sovereignty of the people in pseudonymous newspaper articles by "Publicola." Most readers assumed the elder Adams to be "Publicola," thus heating up the controversy in the newspapers. Privately Adams and Jefferson sought to maintain their friendship, though they could not deny their disagreement. Abigail correctly perceived that James Madison was the moving force behind the Republican opposition and reserved her most severe strictures for him.

The "Discourses on Davila" had been published in John Fenno's *Gazette of the United States*, considered the official organ of the government. In the fall of 1791 Jefferson and Madison encouraged the poet Philip Freneau to take a clerkship in the State Department and begin the *National Gazette* to provide an opposition voice. The contents of these Philadelphia newspapers during the presidential campaign of 1792 reflected two political views, those of the supporters of Washington and Hamilton against a loose coalition opposed to Hamilton's financial system. Both groups considered Washington indispensable, and he reluctantly agreed to a second term. Opponents of the administration concentrated on replacing the Vice President with Governor George Clinton of New York. The *National*

Gazette attacked Adams as an avowed enemy of republicanism who only awaited a suitable moment to subvert the Constitution into a monarchy supported by a horde of new nobles. Jefferson took no public part in the election, and privately advised that his old friend's "personal worth and his services" outweighed the "demerit of his political creed."

In Quincy Abigail recoiled from the "falshood and abuse" heaped on her husband, even though she recognized the real target to be the Secretary of the Treasury. If Hamilton's program fell, she believed, so would the Constitution. Consequently, for her the vice presidential election would determine whether the government of the United States could endure four more years. Despite all the harsh newspaper rhetoric, the national campaign aroused little popular interest. Washington received nearly all the electoral votes and Adams a clear majority of the second ballots, seventy-seven to Clinton's fifty. In Abigail's eyes the election had saved the republic and vindicated the only American statesman "who has had the Courage to point out . . . the Nature and disposition of the humane Heart." She boasted that during the campaign not even the "most virulent party Man of them all" had "dar'd to impeach . . . the Honour, the Honesty, or the integrity of the Vice President."

Abigail took to her bed again in February with the intermitting fever and was bled to relieve her "inflamitory Symptoms." News that the Smiths had safely returned from Europe revived her spirits. Nabby and family had risked a winter voyage to escape the impending war between France and Great Britain. Colonel Smith had switched sides and was now a commercial agent for the French government. Furthermore, his land speculations had brought him some temporary prosperity. John did not know what to make of Nabby's "Adventurer of an Husband" who had become "almost a Revolutionist" and boasted loudly that his newfound wealth freed him from dependence on the petty government jobs Washington had given him. To Abigail John criticized his son-in-law's expensive tastes, and to his face cautioned him against boasting. Nevertheless, he grudgingly respected the colonel's aggressiveness and wished that his own three sons, still dependent on their father's support, had a little more of their brother-in-law's "activity."

Once he knew his reelection to be certain, John wrote to his wife, "Four years more will be as long as I shall have a Taste for public Life or Journeys to Philadelphia. I am determined in the mean time to be no longer the Dupe, and run into Debt to support a vain Post which has

answered no other End than to make me unpopular." He knew that Washington, with a salary
five times the Vice President's, in addition to
house rent and furnishings, had trouble making
ends meet. Abigail long remembered that they
had gone $2,000 into debt during the first vice
presidential term and that she had overworked
in an attempt to save money by preparing food
for guests herself. Though he missed his wife,
John cheered himself with the thought of what
he saved by living in rented rooms. He believed
that he held the "most insignificant office that
ever the Invention of Man contrived or his Imagination conceived." Abigail disagreed sharply,
insisting that from this inactive position he, "like
the Heavenly orbs," silently diffused a "benign
influence" throughout the federal government.
Be assured, she consoled him, the American people "will *one day* do justice to *your Memory.*"

Yet both understood their precarious situation. Her illnesses were the ostensible reason for
Abigail's living in Quincy during John's second
term, while he spent half his time there, away
from the nation's capital. But this pattern made
economic sense and helped to preserve their
health: hers by eliminating trips of a week or
more to Philadelphia and his by keeping him out
of the capital's dangerous hot seasons. That city's
great yellow fever epidemic of 1793 killed five

thousand and turned the former Adams residence at Bush Hill into a paupers' hospital. Law student Tommy Adams joined the wild scramble of the twenty thousand residents fleeing the plague. His mother wanted him to abandon Philadelphia permanently, but he insisted on returning for admission to the bar.

By living in Quincy from March to November 1793, John missed the crisis in relations with France, which had created a republic, executed Louis XVI, declared war on Great Britain and Holland, and commissioned a new minister— Edmond Charles Genêt—to the United States. Citizen Genêt's arrival in the spring of 1793 divided Americans. He rejected Washington's policy of neutrality and appealed directly to Congress and the nation to support France in all ways short of war. In the long run even Jefferson thought it wise to dissociate himself from this undiplomatic rashness, a move that caused John to hope for a moment that the Virginian had at last come to his senses. That hope was dashed when Jefferson resigned from the cabinet at the end of the year, perhaps, John suspected, to improve his chances of succeeding Washington.

John Quincy, bored with writing writs, entered the public controversy surrounding Genêt. Over various pseudonyms he wrote incisive newspaper letters defending the administration's position that the French alliance had ended with the death of the king and that the President had full constitutional authority to dismiss an unacceptable foreign minister. His letters were widely read from Boston to Philadelphia. At twenty-six, Abigail's eldest son suddenly emerged from the obscurity of his law office to become a leading citizen of Boston and to catch the eye of Washington, who welcomed his persuasive defender. Abigail swelled with pride as she wrote to John, "the Time will come when this Young Man will be sought for as a Jewel of great price." She cautioned him, though, that his sons, even John Quincy, still needed their father's counsel: "You will not teach them what to think, but how to think, and they will then know how to act." John saw in his son's compositions a good measure of "his mother's wit" as well as sound political principles.

Abigail did not have long to wait before her son was "sought for." At the end of May 1794 President Washington nominated John Quincy Adams to be minister to the Netherlands, and the Senate concurred unanimously. The father had not the slightest doubt that this son would accept, and dutifully he did. But he wrote in his diary that his father's "satisfaction at the appointment is much greater than mine." He regretted not being consulted "before it was irrevocably made" and was torn between the honor and a feeling of inadequacy for the assignment. Nevertheless, in June John Quincy hastened to Philadelphia to prepare for his mission. He carried a note from his mother to Martha Washington "acknowledging the honor done him by the unsolicited appointment." Abigail added, "At a very early period of Life I devoted him to the publick, . . . and I have the satisfaction to say to you, Madam, perhaps with the fond partiality of a parent, that I do not know in any one Instance of his conduct either at home or abroad, [that] he has given me any occasion of regret."

John Quincy wanted his brother Thomas to accompany him to Holland as his secretary. Though hesitant to leave the law practice he had recently begun in Philadelphia, Tommy yielded to his parents' advice that a young man of twenty-two should not miss this opportunity to see Europe. By November they were in Holland observing the disruption of Europe caused by the French Revolution. When John returned to Philadelphia that same month, Abigail steeled herself to face a lonely winter with no member of her immediate family nearer than New York. Now her anxiety overcame her pride, and she began to lie awake worrying over her sons abroad in "this Whirligig of a World."

She feared most that they would be caught in a war between the United States and Great Britain. American shipping had suffered heavily from the effort of the French and English navies to stop neutral trade. Grievances against the British had so accumulated by 1794 that some American partisans of France clamored for reprisals and even war. Only the tie-breaking vote of the Vice President in the Senate had defeated a non-intercourse bill and, in his judgment, prevented a British declaration of war. John and Abigail rejoiced when Washington chose negotiation rather than battle and sent John Jay to England to seek a settlement. In this crisis the Adamses revealed, as they would during the War of 1812, that, party differences aside, they shared more of Jefferson's than of Hamilton's vision of the future of their country. Abigail advised her husband in words that could have come from Monticello: "The voice of the landed interest is not for War and I dare say it will be found a sound Maxim that the possessors of the soil are the best Judges of what is for the advantage of the Country."

If Jay negotiated a favorable treaty he would become the strongest candidate to succeed Washington. This opinion of John Adams did not weaken his support of the peace mission, for he believed his own political career to be nearing its end. Since Jay had little more bargaining power than Adams in 1784, he came home with a treaty that prevented war but contained few concessions from the British ministry. It took an act of political courage for Washington to submit this unpopular treaty to the Senate for ratification. John returned to Philadelphia from Quincy in June 1795 for the special session that accepted all but the most disliked article. War had been averted, but the unsuccessful effort to undermine the treaty in the House of Representatives made it the main issue of the presidential campaign of 1796. By now two political parties had clearly emerged, the Federalists supporting the administration, and the Republicans in opposition.

Abigail was incensed at the "dishonour and the disgrace" of the "Jacobin" opponents who poured "so much base invective" on Jay and his treaty and even on the President who approved it. This critical moment in the nation's history demanded that the virtuous assume leadership, and she challenged John Quincy to prove himself worthy of his heritage: "You are call'd upon to take a part in this important Business. You have put your hand to the plough, and I know you too well to believe or even wish you to look back or shrink from your duty however arduous or dangerous the task assign'd you. You will prove yourself the Genuine Scion of the Stock from whence you sprang." The hope of the country lay with the leaders of the next generation, Abigail and John agreed as they watched the new extremes of "party spirit, which at best," she concluded, "is but the Madness of the many for the Gain of a few."

When John went to the capital for the special session, Abigail accompanied him as far as New York to see Nabby and Charles. For the moment the Smiths seemed prosperous and happy. Nabby had a new baby to show her mother, who was enchanted with her first granddaughter. Charles also appeared flourishing. His parents had high hope that he had overcome his fondness for dissipation and had turned his brilliance and charm toward making a name at the law. His practice had increased and he had made important friends, among them Hamilton, recently resigned from the cabinet and back in his New York office. For more than a year Charles had been eager to marry, despite his father's warning to be sure of his financial standing first. In August, after his parents had returned home, he married Colonel Smith's sister Sarah, usually called Sally. Nabby seemed relieved that her wayward brother had landed safely in matrimony "after all the Hair Breath scapes and iminent dangers he has run." Months before, Abigail had determined to say nothing to prevent this connection. "Heaven Bless them" was her prayer. For the next two years glowing reports of this son's success lifted a large burden from her mind. After getting to know Sally, Abigail concluded that if Charles reverted to his old habits it would not be his wife's fault.

With John usually home during the growing seasons after 1792, he relieved his wife of much supervision of their scattered farmlands. His attachment to this life became evident when he named the Quincy homestead "Peacefield." From spring to fall, these years were peaceful, happy ones for Abigail despite her infirmities. As always, the relatives entertained each other so frequently that she was never at a loss for intimate company. Her rewarding life contrasted sharply with her younger sister's hardships.

In her Haverhill parish Elizabeth Smith Shaw had displayed personal and intellectual accomplishments equal to those that had drawn attention to Abigail on two continents. She was deeply loved by her Adams nephews, even though while staying with her they had to listen each Sunday to their uncle's sermons full of what John Quincy called "unbending Calvinism." John Shaw died suddenly in 1794, apparently after losing a long if quiet battle with alcohol. He left Elizabeth a near-penniless parson's widow, dependent on the charity of parishioners and relatives. This was her reward for having struggled to raise her three children and to feed the boarders, including Abigail's sons, whom her husband prepared for college. Such a remarkable woman soon attracted at least two widowers, and after a difficult year of widowhood she married Stephen Peabody, minister of Atkinson, New Hampshire. He proved a compatible mate and "one of the warmest advocates for female education." But he also ran a growing academy, much of the work of which fell on his wife. Through it all she set an example of feminine dignity, social grace, and devotion to literary culture. Elizabeth's life reminded Abigail of two lines from Thomas Gray's *Elegy in a Country Churchyard:* "Full many a flower is born to blush unseen, / And waste its sweetness on the desert air." The accident of marriage that had sent William Smith's daughters along such different paths through life was a lesson Abigail understood well. Long since repentant for her initial dislike of John Shaw, she gave generous assistance to his widow and children.

With John entering his sixties and Abigail past fifty, their marriage retained a sensual quality. For example, when she expressed her disapproval of the "January and May" marriage of a young girl to an older man because, among other reasons, it was a union of "the Torrid and the frigid

Zones," John wrote back with pretended indignity: "But how dare you hint or lisp a Word about Sixty Years of Age. If I were near, I would soon convince you that I am not above forty." In such exchanges Abigail disclosed the contentment she felt as she reflected on her married life. On this occasion she wrote, "I would not give up the Heavenly Sensations of a virtuous Love, even at this advanced period of Life, for all the Wealth of all the Indies."

They drew even closer together in periods of indecision or stress, as during the presidential campaign of 1796. By early January John had reliable inside information that Washington would not serve a third term. "You know the Consequence of this, to me and to yourself," he wrote his wife. His vanity was too great to permit serving again as Vice President, especially under Jefferson. But he had little confidence that his reputation and popularity would raise him to the first office.

Abigail's advice followed a familiar pattern. He must do his duty and, as always, she would support him. She herself had little ambition "to be first in Rome," and the prospect of the presidency gave her cause for reflection. She found no "comfort or pleasure in the contemplation" of that possibility. Personal considerations alone would suggest retirement at the same time as

Washington, but "in a Matter of such Momentous concern" she dared not influence her husband. On another question, however, she stood firm: "As to holding an office of Vice President there I will give my opinion. Resign, retire. I would be second unto no Man but Washington."

John clearly wanted the presidency, but only if it came as a recognition of his service and integrity and if he could fill that high office with honor and success. After watching the pitiful example of an aging Samuel Adams serving as governor of Massachusetts, he worried lest he was too old to meet the rigorous demands made of the President. He and his wife had already discussed the certainty that no successor would command the nearly universal respect given Washington. Yet the challenge remained, and John's devotion to duty had not waned with advancing years. He would neither seek the office nor refuse it if elected.

Abigail did not let John fail to consider the part she would be expected to play as First Lady. She doubted that she possessed the "patience, prudence, discretion" of Martha Washington, who had gracefully avoided all controversy. Her own outspokenness might prove detrimental to her President husband: "I should say that I have been so used to a freedom of sentiment that I know not how to place so many guards about me, as will be indispensable, to look at every word before I utter it, and to impose a Silence upon My Self when I long to talk." His reply revealed that he had never fully accepted her freedom of expression in mixed company: "I have no concern on your Account but for your health. A Woman *can* be silent, when she will."

In March, at the end of another winter without her husband, Abigail reminded him again of her greater "sacrifices than any other woman in the Country." He equally valued his public service. From this solid ground of vanity they could either retire to private life, trusting to history to appreciate what a "hard hearted, tyrannical, niggardly Country" had deprived them of; or they could move into the presidency, grateful that the American people always "return to the right path, as soon as they have had time to weigh, consider and reflect."

There had been no public announcement of Washington's retirement by the time John returned to Quincy in May. In this summer of political rumors and intrigue, he busied himself supervising his lands. "Of all the Summers of my Life," he confided to his diary, "this has been the freest from Care, Anxiety and Vexation to me." Abigail suffered some of her chronic complaints, but they did not prevent her from visiting friends in Plymouth and Boston.

The publication of Washington's Farewell Address in mid-September touched off an open campaign. After Jay's harvest of unpopularity from his treaty, the majority of Federalists favored the Vice President, while Jefferson remained the only Republican hope. Although the leading candidates stayed home and made no effort of their own, partisans waged war in the press. The Republicans represented the choice to be between genuine republicanism and hereditary monarchy supported by the aspiring nobles to whom Adams wanted to give titles. The Federalists attacked Jefferson as the atheistic puppet of France, a charge made more plausible when he gained the public support of the new minister from that country. Unwell and alone after John's return to the capital in November, Abigail suffered more from the viciousness of the campaign than her husband. At the end of November she wrote John Quincy, "I fear America will never go through an other Election without Blood Shed. We have had a paper War for six weeks past, and if the Candidates had not themselves been intirely passive, Rage and Violence would have thrown the whole Country into a Flame."

The electoral machinery of the Constitution was unmanageable because the electors, most of them chosen by the state legislatures and only a few by popular vote, met at different times and places to cast their two ballots, one of which must be for a candidate from another state. In February the Vice President opened the official ballots in the presence of Congress, but the results in each state became common knowledge much earlier. This system left an opening for intrigue in the second vote cast by each elector, ostensibly for a Vice President.

The Republicans had no common vice presidential candidate, though Aaron Burr had the most support. Hamilton and the men close to him pushed Thomas Pinckney of South Carolina, who had just negotiated a highly satisfactory treaty with Spain. In December, when Abigail began to receive congratulations on her husband's seemingly certain election, reports reached Quincy that there was a scheme afoot to manipulate the vote to bring in Pinckney ahead of Adams. In Philadelphia John had heard "Insinuations" that Jay had joined Hamilton in this effort. Abigail refused to believe Jay capable of such devious conduct, but Hamilton's "Machiavelian policy" changed her outlook on the election. She reminded John that she had often told him that Hamilton was as "ambitious as Julius Caesar, a subtle intriguer" whose abilities would be dangerous in a mistaken cause, and a man with an insatiable "thirst for Fame." "I have ever kept my Eye upon him," she declared.

John replied in full agreement on the character of Hamilton: "as great an Hypocrite" as there was in the United States and a man of "debauched Morals," though of undoubted talents. Yet John chose not to create an open break in the party by taking notice of "his Puppy hood." Rather, he would continue as always to "keep him at a distance." Fearing her husband might lower his guard against Hamilton, Abigail further warned: "Beware of that Spair Cassius, has always occured to me when I have seen that cock Sparrow. O I have read his Heart in his Wicked Eyes many a time. The very devil is in them. They are laciviousness itself, or I have no Skill in Physiognomy."

Hamilton's reported treachery made both Adamses forget how highly they had once valued his contributions to the new nation. They now much preferred Jefferson for Vice President because Pinckney would be only a puppet of the man who had tried to make him President. Abigail explained to Elbridge Gerry that she retained her friendship for the Virginian and, despite his politics, did "not believe him culpable to the extent he has been represented." She trusted that his conduct as Vice President would be "wise and prudent" and "a means of softning the animosity of party, and of cementing and strengthening the bond of union."

Jefferson had been a most reluctant presidential candidate. When it appeared that the vote would be close, he advised Madison that in case of a tie the Republicans in the House of Representatives should vote for Adams, "who has always been my senior." After he knew Jefferson could not win, Madison published this letter as a gesture of goodwill. Abigail accepted it as the "genuine Sentiments of Mr. Jeffersons Heart." She was correct, for a warm though undelivered congratulatory letter said that he had never doubted the outcome of the election and wished the Adams administration "glory and happiness." Abigail wrote her son that she knew Jefferson to be a man of "strickt honour" who was "incapable of doing a real injury to his Country" and who would never "sacrifice its interests from any pecuniary Motive." On February 8, 1797, the Vice President opened the electoral ballots and announced the results to Congress. He had received seventy-one votes, Jefferson sixty-eight, and Pinckney only fifty-nine. The President and Vice President would be of opposing parties.

In Quincy on this day, Abigail wrote out her prayer for John and described her emotions: "My feelings are not those of pride or ostentation. . . . They are solemnized by a sense of the obligations, the important Trusts and Numerous duties connected with it." And a few days later she promised to curb her tongue in the national interest: "I am my dearest Friend allways willing to be a fellow Labourer with You in all those Relations and departments to which my abilities are competent, and I hope to acquire every requisite degree of Taciturnity which my Station calls for, tho . . . truly . . . it will be putting a force upon Nature."

At home, nevertheless, she did not hesitate to speak her mind freely. She had enrolled her two black servant boys in local schools. When a townsman objected, she delivered him an unanswerable lecture on freedom and equality: "The Boy is a Freeman as much as any of the Young Men, and merely because his Face is Black, is he to be denied instruction, how is he to be qualified to procure a livelihood? Is this the Christian principle of doing to others as we would have others do to us? . . . I have not thought it any disgrace to my self to take him into my parlour and teach him both to read and write. . . . I hope we shall all go to Heaven together."

Abigail did not risk her health by a wintry trip to Philadelphia for the inauguration, and she was determined to make satisfactory arrangements for their Quincy properties before taking her place in the capital. Consequently, the second President took the oath of office on March 4, 1797, without a single member of his family present. Alone with her thoughts on this day, Abigail meditated on a couplet from Edward Young's poetic treatise, *The Love of Fame:*

> High stations tumult, but not bliss, create:
> None think the great unhappy but the great.

At the same time she consoled herself with the words of a hymn she had recently sung with the congregation of the Braintree church:

> Still has my life new wonders seen
> Repeated every year:
> Behold my days that yet remain
> I trust them to thy care.

X

"Fellow Labourer"

1797–1798

The experience of being the President's wife confirmed Abigail Adams in her view of the role of women in republican America. Though she admired the New Jersey constitution of 1776 that permitted a limited number of females to vote, she had no illusions that other states would follow this example (a judgment vindicated when New Jersey disfranchised women in 1807). American wives and mothers could participate in the political process only through private influence on their husbands and sons. At the same time, she stubbornly insisted that the separate roles of the sexes were coordinate and thus of equal importance. While First Lady, she did not mince words on this point: "I will never consent to have our Sex considered in an inferiour point of light. Let each planet shine in

233

their own orbit, God and nature designed it so. If man is Lord, woman is *Lordess*—that is what I contend for, and if a woman does not hold the Reigns of Government, I see no reason for her not judging how they are conducted."

The wife of the President had a unique opportunity to exercise such judgment. John was not only willing that she should be his "fellow Labourer," he insisted upon it. "I never wanted your Advice and assistance more in my Life," he wrote soon after the inauguration. Two weeks later he pleaded, "The Times are critical and dangerous, and I must have you here to assist me." Once he fully understood the burdens of the presidency, he grew desperate for her: "You must come and leave the Place to the mercy of Winds." He needed her to manage the presidential household and to meet his social obligations, but he wanted as much the confidence that he gained from her critical approval. Sixty-two, suffering from tooth and gum disease that impaired his speaking ability, John Adams at times had serious misgivings about his ability which only Abigail could assuage. Awareness of the responsibilities of John's office deepened her own anxiety. His problems were hers. After eight years of vice presidential impotence, John held the "Reigns of Government," and Abigail knew well her duty as a republican woman.

She ignored John's advice to leave their property to the winds; she valued it as an "Ark of Safety" for their retirement and struggled to make the essential arrangements before joining him. He had left her so short of cash that she borrowed the money to appease an impatient tax collector who pressed her with the comment that if the President could not pay his taxes, "who could?" The deaths of her aged mother-in-law and a young niece delayed the departure until the end of April. Her party of thirteen—including servants and the two nieces for whom she cared—set off in two carriages, accompanied on the first short leg of the journey by a delegation of proud friends and neighbors from Quincy. After a week of rain and mud, she stopped for a day at East Chester, New York, where Nabby now lived on an isolated farm. She then visited Charles briefly in New York City before heading for Philadelphia. On May 10 the President met her twenty-five miles outside the capital, and they drove together to her new home.

The Georgian house designated as the presidential mansion had seemed magnificent in colonial days, but the first President had found it uncomfortably small for his needs. It irritated John no end that the city corporation of Philadelphia not only expected the chief executive to pay rent for this mansion but charged him twice what Washington had paid. He also grumbled at

Washington's servants for leaving the scant furnishings provided by Congress in the "most deplorable Condition." John had been initially overwhelmed by the expenses of his office: in addition to house rent, out of his own pocket came the cost of carriages, horses, servants, and a private secretary; and the President was expected to contribute to every charity. He feared that inflation had so reduced the value of his $25,000 annual salary that four years in office would throw him into bankruptcy. Congress refused to raise the salary but did grudgingly make a small appropriation for furnishings. Under Abigail's firm hand, supported as always by their faithful majordomo, John Briesler, the Adamses not only lived within their income but saved several thousand to invest. By contrast, Washington had drawn on private funds to meet presidential expenses, and Jefferson would leave office heavily in debt.

Abigail had written to Martha Washington for advice on how she might emulate "her most amiable predecessor" whose conduct as First Lady had been so "exemplary" and "irreproachable." Mrs. Washington replied with equal flattery and modestly fulfilled the request for her social rules. The contrast between the wives of the first and second Presidents was sharp. Martha, devoted entirely to the comfort of her husband,

exhibited little interest in or ability to understand the momentous issues of national life. She
was notable only for being noncontroversial. Experienced in European courts, Abigail knew how
to entertain elegantly, albeit with a concern for
frugality foreign to the plantation style of
Mount Vernon. More noticeable, dinners at the
republican court of the Adamses were sparked
by stimulating and entertaining conversation, in
which the irrepressible hostess took a leading
part, while guests at the Washington dinner table
were often awed into silence by the dignity of
the President and the bland pleasantness of his
First Lady.

Dozens of callers descended on Abigail while she
tried to recover from her journey and get the mansion in order. She decided to postpone a regular
drawing-room reception until the refurnishing
could be completed in the fall, but immediately uti-
lized her dining room for a round of dinners with
as many as forty guests at one time. After dining at
the President's, one congressman wrote, "Mrs.
Adams conducted herself with the greatest propriety. The dinner was genteel, without profusion; the
wine rather mediocre."

Abigail dreaded the approach of July 4. The
first President had set the expensive precedent of
celebrating this national holiday with a reception
for a host of officials and Philadelphians. This

year, for the first time, Congress would be in session, adding one hundred and fifty to the company. But after privately censuring Washington for "introducing the custom," Abigail was gratified that the Independence Day festivity went well as she and the President separately received guests from noon until four o'clock. Her initial trepidation rapidly vanished, and she began to take pleasure in her public role as First Lady.

Yet Abigail's greatest satisfaction came from her private role as confidant of, counselor to, and defender of the President. Standing at the center of the nation's political life, she felt the obligation of republican womanhood more strongly than ever before. Her intense concern with the single critical issue dominating the administration of John Adams proved debilitating. She could never rest while her husband's fame—and hers—hung in the balance.

The election of a Federalist President and a Republican Vice President gave the nation a few weeks of political peace. Then quickly the threat of war with France rekindled party passions. The French government, now in the hands of a five-man executive called the Directory, had authorized the plundering of American shipping and taken other hostile actions against the nation it considered to be an ungrateful ally. When the Directory insultingly refused to receive the minister sent by Washington and stepped up the war on American commerce, the President called a special session of Congress to consider the crisis. The early widespread support for his effort to find a diplomatic solution eroded over the composition of a commission to negotiate with the Directory. Adams wanted a nonpartisan commission; but after Jefferson and Madison declined to serve, he gave in to the demands of his cabinet and nominated three Federalists: John Marshall of Virginia; Charles C. Pinckney, the repudiated minister; and Francis Dana, chief justice of Massachusetts.

In one of her most elegant and revealing letters, Abigail rushed the news of Dana's appointment to his wife. She refused to entertain the slightest doubt that her good friend Mrs. Dana would not answer the call of patriotic duty by sacrificing her domestic bliss to the nation's security. Who, she made clear, had a better right to ask such a sacrifice than herself? For reasons of health, Dana declined, but his wife retained the First Lady's respect because she had "not thrown any discouragement in the way of Mr. Dana's acceptance."

The President now defied his Federalist advisers by replacing Dana with the man he had wanted in the first place—Elbridge Gerry, a Massachusetts politician personally loyal to him but too stubbornly independent to align himself

with either party. Since Gerry was regarded as a
friend of France, this nomination angered the extreme Federalists. Abigail had corresponded with
Gerry off and on for many years. The day his acceptance arrived in Philadelphia, she wrote to express her "great pleasure," but obliquely cautioned him against being so "tenacious" in his
opinions as to defeat the unanimity the commission needed in negotiations.

The special session of Congress adjourned on
July 8 after voting some feeble preparations for
war. Its wake churned with distrust and personal
abuse. The Republicans believed they had prevented the Federalists from declaring war on
France as part of a plot to secure British aid in
restoring monarchy and aristocracy to the
United States. Extreme Federalists countered
with charges of cowardice in the face of France's
spoliation of American shipping. Uninhibited
partisan writers had revealed Jefferson to be a
slanderer of Washington, and Hamilton an adul-
terer. Abigail strained to preserve her dignity as
she read the Republican press. She was most af-
fronted by the "abuse and scurility" of the
Philadelphia *Aurora,* edited by Franklin's grandson, Benjamin Franklin Bache, who had been
John Quincy's schoolmate in France. Yet according to the wife of the British ambassador, the
new First Lady had "spirit enough to laugh at

Baches Abuse of her Husband, which poor Mrs. Washington could not."

Two months in the capital confirmed Abigail's long-held opinion that Philadelphia was a hotbed of foreign revolutionaries—"Jacobins," she called them—who, "having forfeited the priviledges of their own Country," now sought "to embroil and destroy" the free American republic that had given them asylum. Most distressing of all, the evidence was inescapable that Jefferson was emerging from retirement at Monticello to lead the Republican opposition. Abigail blamed his actions on defects of mind rather than of heart, a view that brought only slight solace.

She heartily approved the President's decision to escape the capital's yellow fever and "Bake House" heat by spending the remainder of the summer and the early fall in Quincy. The journey proved difficult, the heat made more oppressive by successive clouds of dust and rain. One crowded inn could do no better for the President's wife than a thin mattress on the floor, but generally they were pleased and a little surprised at the military and civil honors shown them on the trip. Once home, they were besieged with more honors and a stream of company. The President had to stay close to Quincy to read and answer daily his official correspondence, but Abigail was freer to visit friends and relatives.

Except for minor injuries suffered in a carriage accident, she enjoyed one of the most rewarding summers of her life. If only the capital of the United States could have been Boston, her satisfaction would have been complete.

But back to Philadelphia they went in October 1797. Along the road citizens of all ranks again turned out to greet the President, whose plain manners and lack of regal display gave the lie to charges that he favored aristocracy. Abigail took heart to see that "the people will love and respect their Chief Magistrate, if his administration is that of wisdom and justice." At East Chester, where they stopped to visit Nabby, word arrived that yellow fever plagued Philadelphia. As a result, they delayed their return to the capital for nearly a month.

East Chester held little joy for Abigail. Colonel Smith had purchased this farm, twenty miles from New York City, for a summer retreat while he began building a permanent residence near the city. He had planned the new house on such a grand scale that neighbors soon referred to it as "Smith's folly." Such it was, for in 1796 his straw empire of speculation, loans, and bad investments had collapsed. Forced to halt construction of his mansion, he had sacrificed some of his land in an effort to settle out of court a suit brought by a creditor. Then Smith had gone

to salvage what he could from his land speculations in the wilds of western New York. Left
with a bare subsistence, Nabby had put up a
brave front, but to her brother she expressed
doubts that she could retain her sanity. When
Abigail reached East Chester, Nabby had not
heard from her husband for four months and
knew nothing of his whereabouts.

Abigail now sadly judged her dashing son-in-
law to have been a good soldier but otherwise
"wholy devoid of judgment." She had already
assumed responsibility for the education of his
two sons by placing them under her sister's care
in the academy at Atkinson. Here they would be
removed from the permissive society of Nabby's
in-laws and would have the advantage of a
"Genuine New England education," which, Abigail boasted, was the best she had seen in Europe
or America.

Nabby's unfortunate marriage had resulted
from a whirlwind romance in London. Another
London marriage might bring the same unhappi-
ness to the oldest Adams son. This thought had
troubled Abigail ever since she had learned of
John Quincy's engagement to Louisa Catherine
Johnson, daughter of the United States consul in
London and his English wife. Remembering his
parents' objections to his earlier romance, Johnny
had at first only hinted to them of his affection for

Louisa Catherine, while making plain his determination to follow his own heart and head. Nearing thirty, with ten years of diplomatic experience behind him, he was at last his own man.

From the outset his mother acknowledged his maturity. Even before she knew for certain the identity of his intended, she wrote: "You have Years sufficient to judge for Yourself, and whom you call yours shall be mine also, only weigh well, consider maturely of the most important action of your Life." Having known the opulent Johnson family in England, Abigail worried lest her prospective daughter-in-law might be spoiled by luxury and a European education. Her accomplishments "both in mind and person" had made her fit to grace a court but may not have fitted her "for the discharge of those domestic duties which cement the union of Hearts, and give it its sweetest pleasures." Johnny's reassurances somewhat calmed his mother's fears. If anything, he half-seriously complained, Louisa, though eight years younger than himself, was the more cautious and prudent of the two.

The marriage in London during July 1797 was widely announced in the newspapers. President Washington had promoted the young diplomat by naming him minister to Portugal, but before he could reach that post his President father had given him the more desirable appointment to

Prussia. The Republican press had cried "Nepotism"—the "American Prince of Wales" had been given a sinecure to complete his European education—and the marriage gave the editors more ammunition. An unfriendly Boston newspaper scoffed that "Young John Adams's negotiations have terminated in a marriage treaty with an English lady, . . . It is a happy circumstance that he had made no other Treaty."

When the presidential party finally reached Philadelphia in the middle of November, the Republican press greeted them with new salvos of scurrility. Abigail took particular offense at Bache's assertion that displays of respect for the "Duke of Braintree," as he dubbed the President, had been forced rather than spontaneous. Having seen "many affecting proofs" of genuine respect and affection, she knew better. She succeeded in several private efforts to have material favorable to the President, including extracts on European affairs from her sons' letters, inserted in newspapers. But most of all she longed for legal authority to curb the licentious press and cleanse the country of foreign agitators.

Abigail and John passed the winter of 1797–1798 in suspenseful anticipation of hearing from the commissioners to France. Bache characterized them at this time as "The Happy Old Couple" of the English ballad "Darby and

Joan," too retired for anything more active than pleasure in each other's company. But a Federalist newspaper editor turned this slur on the chief executive's capacity to govern into a compliment "to the domestic and conjugal Character of the President who has never given His Children or Grandchildren cause to Blush for any illegitimate offspring"—an obvious comparison with the reputed private life of Jefferson.

Upper-class Philadelphians enjoyed a full social life during these winter months, but it centered in private mansions to which the Adamses were largely strangers. Abigail held her Friday evening drawing room for the ladies, John received gentlemen at a Monday daytime levee, and the presidential dining table seated guests almost daily. Typically, though, members of Congress, the diplomatic corps, or personal friends attended these affairs more often than the leaders of Philadelphia society. During Washington's years in office, his birthday celebration, a glittering ball for as many as a thousand people, had climaxed the social season. President Adams firmly rejected an invitation to the ball on the first February 22 of the new administration. He considered it an affront to his office. And there were rumors that Hamilton's friends had promoted the event to make the President's refusal appear a slight to Washington.

Privately Abigail fumed at the Philadelphia socialites who pretended "to give Laws of politeness and propriety to the union" but had less "feeling of real genuine politeness of any people" she knew. How could the President attend a ball for "private citizen" Washington except in a "secondary character" that would lower his office in the eyes of foreign nations! The sponsors of such festivities should learn "what belongs to the Character of the Head of our Nation," a lesson taught them by the sparse attendance at the ball. Even Jefferson, out of deference to Adams, declined an invitation. The following January Philadelphia gave a ball for Adams, which satisfied protocol and opened the way for him to attend Washington's birthday celebration in February.

Abigail Adams, daughter of a Quincy, presented at the courts of Versailles and Saint James, wife and confidant of the President of the United States, could not be intimidated by high society in this city for which she had so little fondness. She boasted that in her "drawing room is frequently to be seen an assemblage of as much Beauty and elegance, as is to be met with in any foreign Court." More vital, she soon began to see evidence that even Philadelphians appreciated her husband's wisdom and prudence.

For months Abigail had eagerly seized upon every scintilla of support for her husband. She was convinced that if he failed the resultant crisis in foreign affairs would terminate the unnatural union of the regions that had formed the nation: "I hope we may be held together, but I know not how long, for oil and water are not more contrary in their Nature than North and South." She feared that America would be punished because a party in its Congress supported France's diabolic crusade to subject the world to its anti-Christian tyranny. Only the might of Great Britain stood in the way of total French victory. She thus began to forgive the former mother country its past sins.

Early in March 1798 the first dispatches from the commissioners reached the President, and their contents soon became public knowledge. The Directory had insulted the United States by refusing officially to receive the emissaries and privately—through secret agents designated by Adams only as X, Y, Z—had demanded a large bribe to enter upon negotiations. Public opinion rallied in support of the President's appeal for war preparations. Abigail rejoiced at the "cementing of Hearts, and the union of mind." To her sons in Europe she rushed the news of the alteration that had "taken place in this City, the center of foreign influence and Jacobinism."

While the "unprincipled Jacobin" remained "unchanged," the common people, hitherto "deceived, and betray'd by falshood" were "uniting and united." Abigail's drawing room was now packed. As she rode through the streets of Philadelphia, people of all ranks bowed or removed their hats. Even the Quakers noticed her "*in their way.*" "In short," she wrote her sister, "we are now wonderfully popular except with Bache & Co who in his paper calls the President old, querilous, Bald, blind, cripled, Toothless Adams."

In April she enjoyed one of her most satisfying moments as First Lady when she attended the theater incognito to hear the first public rendition of "Hail Columbia," a patriotic song set to the tune of the "President's March." In the past, French revolutionary songs had been applauded when sung from this same stage; but on this night the audience demanded four encores of "Hail Columbia" and showed appreciation with cheers that Abigail thought could be heard a mile away.

Republicans had sometimes flaunted on their hats the tricolor cockade (a rosette of ribbon) worn by the French revolutionaries. After the XYZ revelations Federalists and patriots countered with the black cockade of the American Revolution. In May Abigail watched with delight as "near Eleven Hundred" young men of

Philadelphia, wearing black cockades, paraded through the President's "levee Room" to display their willingness to defend the country. One report had the First Lady herself presenting black cockades to a delegation calling on her husband. The city quickly became unsafe for wearers of the French cockade.

While the President spent long hours at his desk replying to the formal addresses of support from various groups of citizens, his wife wrote letter after letter to alert her circle to the crisis. In the spring of 1798 she believed that a state of war existed, even if undeclared, and that if a declaration of war was required to sound the call to arms, "the sooner the better." The time had come to show the French that "we did not break from the shackels of our parent, to become slaves of our sister, a venal, depraved, corrupt and proffligate wretch, who has rejected our profered terms of reconciliation, and calls for bribes." Though war was "a dreadful scourge to any country," subjugation was worse, "particularly so to France." By June she gave full credence to the widely rumored French scheme for the conquest of America. Her letter warned a nephew at Harvard College that the plan was settled. After taking Louisiana, Florida, and Canada, French arms would turn against the United States, foment a slave rebellion, and sow atheistic principles throughout the country, destroying the religious and political foundations of this free people. "It becomes every individual to rise, and unite, to stop the progress, to arrest the poison before it contaminates our vitals."

Abigail's fears were widely shared in New England, where the clergy had sounded the alarm in sermon after sermon. She eagerly embraced the thesis of the eminent Scottish scientist John Robison, whose *Proofs of a Conspiracy against all the Religions and Governments of Europe,* published the year before, confirmed all she had heard and suspected concerning the transplantation of French atheistic tyranny to America. In these pages she found "proof that Religion and Government are so intimately connected, that it is impossible for them to stand seperately and alone." As a result, it was "impossible for honesty and truth to reside in the Breast of a Jacobin." The Republicans, with the sadly deceived Jefferson at their head, had fallen so completely under "Jacobin" influence that they could no longer distinguish right from wrong. Even the "Common People," she believed, understood that "if J[efferson] had been our President, and Madison and Burr our Negotiators, we should all have been sold to the French."

By early summer 1798, Abigail wanted Congress to declare war as a means of rallying the American people against foreign subversion. She denounced her friend Gerry for remaining in France to conduct secret negotiations after the other two commissioners had left. His "unaccountable stay," she wrote her son, had been a check on a declaration of war which "ought undoubtedly to have been made." But most of all, President Adams delayed asking for a declaration of war because "the Majority in Congress did not possess firmness and decision enough to boldly make it."

Congress did set the stage for an undeclared naval war by creating the Department of the Navy, enlarging the fleet, authorizing it to seize armed French vessels on the high seas, and granting the President the authority to commission privateers. An embargo cut off trade with the ally-turned-enemy. Congress also tripled the regular army and provided for a sizable reserve in case of an actual land war. President Adams placed his faith in the "Wooden Walls" of the navy and had little enthusiasm for a large army. As it turned out, though, the creation of an army had important political consequences. To thwart Hamilton's desire to head the army, Adams nominated Washington, who reluctantly agreed to come out of retirement on condition that Hamilton be second in command. In the struggle over Hamilton's rank, Adams for the first time faced squarely the unpleasant truth that the three key members of his cabinet gave their primary allegiance to the former Secretary of the Treasury.

Abigail watched the powerful interest behind Hamilton's military leadership with mixed feelings. He would "make an able and active officer" but she feared that he might become the American Napoleon Bonaparte. He was a man driven by ambition without the check of virtue. At the head of the army, he, like Napoleon, could use military force to overpower the government and launch a series of invasions of neighboring lands to acquire an empire. For her, as for the President, Washington's service in this crisis as a watchdog over the would-be Napoleon was "of much more concequence and importance now, than it was in our Revolution."

Given a larger army than he had wanted, John Adams saw in it at least an opportunity to redeem his son-in-law. Though uneasy over the colonel's business practices, he could not entertain the idea that Nabby's husband was dishonorable. Washington agreed to Smith's appointment as a brigadier general but preferred that he be given a command in the line. Instead, the President insisted on nominating him to be adjutant general of the army, a staff position just below Hamilton, the inspector general. By the time the military appointments reached the Senate floor, the senators were so well informed of Smith's reputation as a bankrupt speculator and political opportunist that he received few votes. Hamilton's men in the cabinet had advised the Senate to reject him, to save the President from the political consequences of his blindness, they maintained. Abigail acknowledged that the colonel's reputation had resulted from "his own folly and indiscretion"; still she believed that her husband's opposition to Hamilton lay behind the rejection of a good and brave soldier, qualified for no other career, who would be crushed by this disappointment.

John and Abigail saw no harm in appointing qualified relatives to federal offices; their country owed them a debt for past services. Yet the President had established a policy of removing no officeholder except for cause and appointing no one not well recommended and above suspicion. As word of the First Lady's presumed influence spread, she had received frequent appeals from job seekers, which she had answered in a high-principled tone. But in the case of their son-in-law, neither could accept his unsavory reputation. The Republican press vigorously pressed the charge of nepotism, with more substance this time than in the case of John Quincy; and the Hamiltonian Federalists saw new evidence of the President's poor judgment.

For months Abigail had criticized congressional inaction and timidity. At last, in the final weeks of the session, Congress passed acts aimed at aliens and at the unrestrained press. The Alien Acts frightened a few non-citizens into leaving, but otherwise had few consequences. Still they lent credence to her view that "most of our troubles in this Country arise from imported foreigners." The Sedition Act became the chief instrument of the drive to muzzle the most objectionable Republican editors. Though the President had not asked Congress for this legislation, he signed the bills with no hesitation. His wife's zealous advocacy of these measures belied his attempt in later life to dodge the responsibility for what most of his countrymen by then considered repressive legislation.

The French example proved to Abigail that a press left free to heap abuse on government inevitably created political chaos. In the United States, she had concluded, "the Liberty of the press is become licentious beyond any former period." She had faith that "the Good sense of the American people in general directs them Right, where they can see and judge for themselves." But they could not judge rightly when fed a steady diet of journalistic "abuse, deception and falshood" that destroyed the "confidence and Harmony which is the Life Health and Security of a Republic."

Her view of the freedom of the press was self-serving and partisan. She had forgotten her earlier resentment of the vicious attacks on Jefferson by

Federalist editors no less licentious than Bache. Yet her position was understandable, concerned as she was with preserving the republic from the extremes of mobocracy and despotism. Any right-thinking patriot would prefer the moderate government of Washington and Adams to the Reign of Terror and the Directory. The nation was fighting an undeclared war with France, the country whose military might threatened American sovereignty and whose social and moral influence menaced society. Even so, the Sedition Act was milder than a similar law in Britain. Congress had also declared void the treaties of 1778 with France. The First Lady rejoiced that the legislators had finally awakened to the nation's peril.

In July Abigail found Philadelphia's "extreem heat" so unbearable that she could not "eat, sleep, read, write or do any thing but labour to breathe." Soon after the congressional session ended, she and the President set out for Quincy, stopping at East Chester to take Nabby with them. Demonstrations of support repeatedly delayed their journey, and in nearly every town mounted escorts raised a cloud of dust on dirt roads baked by near-one-hundred-degree temperatures. They listened—and John replied—to addresses of welcome and to the popular new patriotic song, "Adams and Liberty," sung to the tune later used for "The Star Spangled Banner." Its last stanza began with words that echoed the image of her husband broadcast in Abigail's letters:

> Let Fame to the world sound America's voice;
>   No intrigues can her sons from their government
>   sever;
> Her pride is her Adams; her laws are his choice,
>   And shall flourish, till Liberty slumbers for ever.

On August 8 Abigail arrived home exhausted and ill. Suffering from a vaguely defined bilious disorder accompanied by an "intermitting fever," she soon sank so low that physicians and family despaired of her life. As she lay for weeks on what she believed to be her deathbed, she gave thanks for Nabby's loving presence and entrusted John with her blessing for their absent sons who would never see their mother again.

XI

"What I Cannot Remedy"

1798–1801

For eleven weeks Abigail did not leave her bed-chamber. Her symptoms suggest a half dozen diagnoses, with a good possibility being amoebic dysentery, complicated by the intermitting fever, probably a flare-up of malaria. For once she spared her correspondents the details of the bloodlettings, blisters, powders, and exotic diets her physicians prescribed. By the middle of November she had recovered from the near-fatal ailment, though the fever remained and chronic insomnia left her weak for months. Her sleeplessness may have resulted from anxiety over her family and the nation; in any case, it slowed a return to physical well-being.

Illness diminished Abigail's pleasure in the homecoming surprise she had planned for John. Without telling him, she had ordered extensive remodeling of their Quincy house, the first project being a library-office with an outside entrance, where he could house his books and conduct business. A Quincyite visiting Philadelphia had let the secret slip to John, who enjoyed a "hearty laugh" over his wife's independent management. In his new study the President attended to the nation's affairs whenever he could tear himself away from her sickbed. But he had difficulty keeping his mind on the duties of his office, for, as she later observed, the possibility of her death "more closely bound" them "to each other."

It was a fortunate time to be in the relative isolation of the Quincy farm. Soon after the Adamses left, yellow fever broke out in Philadelphia and spread northward. The federal capital had to be moved temporarily to Trenton again. Four of Abigail's Philadelphia servants died from the plague, which also carried off, in a display of political neutrality, the rival newspaper editors John Fenno and Benjamin Bache.

In September the British ambassador came to Quincy to offer an alliance against France. President Adams expressed interest without making a commitment. By then his war fever had begun to abate. He now feared that Hamilton and the extreme Federalists would expand a war into a crusade to capture Louisiana and liberate Spain's American colonies. A letter from John Quincy in Europe to his mother indicated that the Directory appeared more conciliatory. In October Gerry belatedly returned from France and came to Quincy with the same message, which later reports further confirmed. By the end of the month the President had new hope that an honorable peace might be possible.

John set off for Philadelphia the second week in November; yet his thoughts stayed behind in Quincy. After a day on his journey he wrote Abigail, "If I had less Anxiety about your health, I should have more about public affairs, I suppose." Her sorrow at their separation was intensified by feelings of guilt because she would not be at her post beside the President. At first Nabby proposed to nurse her mother through the winter. But when Abigail saw her daughter torn between duty to parent and husband, she sent her flying after John to catch him on the road and travel with him as far as East Chester. Once again Abigail faced a winter's cold and isolation without a member of her family nearby.

Abigail joked with John that she could "be but a half way politician this winter." Nevertheless, she insisted that he keep her fully informed of developments in the capital. He did, with the help of William Shaw, a nephew he had taken back with him as a private secretary. One of Shaw's first letters cheered her with the news that a volunteer light infantry company from Hampshire County, Massachusetts, had petitioned to be organized under the name of the "Lady Adams Rangers."

The President's annual message to Congress in December 1798 urged continued preparation for war but expressed a willingness to negotiate whenever France stood ready to receive a minister. By February he believed this condition had been met. Without consulting his cabinet—not even Timothy Pickering, the Secretary of State and chief Hamilton supporter in the administration— he appointed a peace mission headed by William Vans Murray, the American minister to Holland, through whom had come some of France's conciliatory gestures. This move stunned and angered the Hamiltonians. Some attributed it to the President's senility and others to the absence of his wife, who a few months before had been so belligerent toward France. She, they believed, was the only person from whom this stubborn old man still took advice. Amused, he wrote from Philadelphia, "Oh how they lament Mrs. Adams's Absence! She is a good Counsellor! If she had been here Murray would never have been named nor his Mission instituted." From Boston Abigail learned that "some of the Feds who did not like being taken so by surprise, said they wisht the old Woman had been there; they did not believe it would have taken place."

Although Abigail knew and approved of John's growing desire to avoid war, his naming a new minister to France caught her, like the nation, by surprise. She rose to the occasion by assuring him that it did not "in the least flatter my vanity, to have the public Imagine that I am not equally pacific with my Husband, or that the same Reasons and Motives, which led him to take upon his own shoulders the weight, of a measure, which he knew must excite a Clamour, would not have equally opperated upon my mind, if I had been admitted a partner in the Counsel." Nevertheless, she had "not any very sanguine expectation of success" for this "master stroke of policy" which "puts to the test the sincerity of the Directory." She denied her influence on the President and insisted that she had "never pretended to the weight" ascribed to her, whereupon she promptly advised him not to heed the congressional demand to add others to the peace mission.

Signs of popular resistance to the direct land tax, commonly known as the window tax, levied to support the army, had worried the President.

The month after he left, Abigail experienced at first hand what this tax meant when the local assessors visited her to measure all buildings, "count every square of Glass," calculate the area of all land, and finally appraise the whole. When they finished she made certain that they did not think it proper to increase her assessment in order to give the President the honor of having "the best House in Town." Abigail and John sensed that taxes were overtaking foreign affairs as the vital political issue. Open rebellion in Pennsylvania during the coming spring proved them correct.

Abigail had known for months that Tommy was on his way home. When he had not arrived by the end of 1798, her fears of a winter Atlantic crossing increased her insomnia. Both parents suffered periods of depression this winter: Tommy might have been lost at sea, and Charles had grown strangely silent concerning the money Johnny had left with him to invest. Nabby's husband had further embarrassed the President. John had urged Smith not to accept the command of a regiment because his military experience entitled him to a higher rank than colonel and because his "pride and ostentation" had made him the target for charges of "dishonorable and dishonest conduct" from his father-in-law's political enemies. But Smith wanted the appointment and the President reluctantly obliged him. Once again a protracted debate laid bare Smith's shoddy reputation, though this time the Senate confirmed him after "warm opposition." John considered this one of the low points of his life. Colonel Smith's pay as a regimental commander, his father-in-law grumbled, "will not feed his Dogs: and his Dogs must be fed if his children starve." He poured out his soul to Abigail: "Happy Washington! happy to be Childless! My Children give me more Pain than all my Enemies."

Abigail gently rebuked him: "I do not consider GW at all a happier man because he has not children. If he has none to give him pain, he has none to give him pleasure. . . . Vicious conduct will always be a source of disquietude to me, [but] if my wishes are blasted I must submit to it, as a punishment, a trial, an affliction which I must bear and what I cannot remedy I must endure." They were fast approaching old age, a time of their lives in which "no pleasure is to be found" except as religion supplied "the insufficiency of worldly pleasures." Perhaps with Jefferson in mind, she continued: "Who would exchange these Consolations for the cold comfortless prospect of the Materilist?" Even if the Christian religion is in error, "it is one which raises us above the Bruits, it exalts and enobles our faculties, and the deception if it were one, can do us no injury."

Tommy's safe landing at New York in January 1799 lifted some of the gloom hanging over his parents. He went directly to Philadelphia to bring his father reports from France. Abigail waited impatiently for him in Quincy, though she warned that "he must prepare to see his mother ten years older than when he left her; time and sickness have greatly altered her." Their happy reunion took place in February. Abigail required only two days to conclude that her youngest son had "returned to his Native Country an honest, sober and virtuous citizen." Against his mother's wishes, Tommy made plans to settle in Philadelphia and study law. Neither parent thought him cut out for the legal profession. Abigail urged him to remain home and enter business: three lawyers in one family were enough, especially when none had grown wealthy at the law. Tommy persisted, nevertheless, and his departure for Philadelphia in the spring marked the psychological weaning of Abigail's last child.

At the beginning of April 1799, the President returned to Quincy and remained there until October. He needed time to measure the impact of his foreign policy on the American public and on the British, now celebrating Admiral Nelson's great victory over the French at the Battle of the Nile. Meanwhile, the ships of the new American navy were nearing completion. Two commissioners were designated to join Murray, but Adams almost winked at Secretary Pickering's frantic intrigues to delay their sailing. Abigail's continued frailty provided a convenient excuse to John for biding his time, while he was, in his wife's words, holding "the sword in one hand and the olive Branch in the other."

During the winter Abigail had continued to encourage editors to publish items meeting her approval. She had dismissed the resolutions of the Virginia and Kentucky legislatures against the Alien and Sedition Acts as "foreign influence . . . united with domestic intrigue." She had harsh words for Federalist John Marshall's opposition to those acts and kind words for Gerry after he had satisfactorily explained his behavior to the President. Now with John home, she caught up on the information too confidential to be entrusted to the mails. After a brief relapse with the onset of hot weather, she grew stronger. By July she was giving dinners to compensate for her inactivity of the previous summer and had entered the political mainstream with all her former vigor.

In writing to John Quincy at the end of July, Abigail's pen dripped euphoria. Her health was better and the land was green. A show of force had suppressed the anti-tax insurrection in Pennsylvania. The new frigates, the *Constitution* and the *Boston,* were at sea. These wooden walls were "the objects which the President has most nearly at Heart: he may really be call'd the Father of them." From the English, the French were at last "receiving the measure which they have meeted to others." The President enjoyed excellent health and continued "firm as a Rock, tho the Waves sometimes beat and the Bellows roar." Abigail was not in the least defensive over her husband's absence from the capital for these six months. The mail took only four days, and he answered his official correspondence daily. "When the President thinks it necessary for him to be at Philadelphia he will go, but not an hour before to please friends or silence foes."

The one black cloud in Abigail's otherwise beautiful summer sky floated over Charles in New York City. At last she and John had to face the bitter truth that their most personable son, despite his talents and advantages, was slipping into dissipation and dishonor. According to his mother, his character contained a fatal flaw: he "never had the power of resistance." Now she sorrowfully acknowledged that she had given birth to a "graceless child."

John Quincy had entrusted Charles with $6,000, and possibly more, to invest on commission according to "precise instructions." For more than two years Charles had failed to provide an accounting or even to answer letters asking for one. Eventually he reported to his mother that he had diverted the money to save his brother-in-law Colonel Smith from debtors prison. This "apologetic account," Tommy soon discovered, "was very far from being the whole truth." On his way back to the capital in October 1799, the President stopped in New York to see for himself. For the first time Sally Adams revealed the full extent of her husband's alcoholism and indebtedness. The facts were sufficient to cause the father to brand his son "a Madman possessed of the Devil," a "Rake" and a "Beast," a "Reprobate" who "shall be punished." To Abigail John declared with finality, "I renounce him," but the mother could never forsake a child of hers however great the sorrow he caused her.

Alcohol was proving to be the curse of the Adams family—first Abigail's brother William, then her brother-in-law John Shaw, now her son Charles, and in time her son Thomas and other close relatives. In this "Alcoholic Republic," as one historian described the new nation, nearly all men drank a variety of alcoholic beverages in quantity. John Adams, though fond of hard cider himself, had once unsuccessfully tried to limit the number of taverns in Braintree. Business was often conducted in inns, taverns, or men's social clubs. New Yorkers, among whom Charles had settled, were known as especially heavy drinkers. Abigail's frequent admonitions against intemperance came from a mother well aware of the social pitfalls her sons faced. Of the three, only John Quincy developed the sterling character that enabled him to drink regularly without being consumed by alcohol.

It was a grieving, bitter President who traveled to Trenton for an emergency meeting of his cabinet. The First Lady followed a few days behind, planning to wait at East Chester until Philadelphia was clear of yellow fever and the government had returned there. At Nabby's she found Sally Adams and her two daughters taking refuge from the plague in New York City and from an intemperate husband and father there. Abigail and Nabby left early in November. They visited Colonel Smith at his New Jersey army camp and then joined the President for the remaining miles to Philadelphia.

When John Adams reached Trenton, he found Hamilton there to join in the argument against the peace mission. The President did not budge and instead decided that the time had come to dispatch the commissioners. His order to this effect on October 16 marked a sharp break with the Hamiltonians. By a calm annual message to Congress in December, he attempted to place himself with the mass of patriotic citizens in the center between Federalist militarism and imported radicalism.

Abigail moved step by step with her husband toward peace. She no longer considered Great Britain the bulwark against the French Revolution and now believed that the long-existing English jealousy of American prosperity would lead that government to promote continued friction between the United States and France. President Adams, she insisted, was not closely tied to British interests as were the extreme Federalists but sought to render his nation "independent of foreign attachments" altogether. Americans could no longer expect from Englishmen only the "monarchial hatred of Republicanism" she had experienced at Whitehall. Now English radicals fleeing from that kingdom to the United States brought with them their "democratic madness." In the last few months Thomas Cooper had flared into prominence with his public attacks on the Adams administration. An English revolutionary who had become a naturalized citizen, Cooper provided one more illustration for Abigail of the folly of her country's "becoming an assylum for the turbulent and discontented spirits of other nations." America's salvation lay in ridding itself of foreign influence, whether from Paris or London.

In response to the death of Washington in December 1799, the nation appeared to draw together for a few weeks. Abigail's drawing room was crowded with two hundred ladies in stylish mourning gowns. She refused a request to fix an official period of mourning in the style of the English court, though she kept her family in black until spring and then "put on half mourning." Her note of sympathy to Martha Washington was eloquently simple: "I intreat Madam, that You would permit a Heart deeply penetrated with your loss, and sharing personally in Your Grief, to mingle with You, the Tears which flow for the partner of all Your joys and sorrows." Nonetheless, Abigail saw a danger in the hundreds of exaggerated eulogies for Washington. By building him into a godlike savior of his country, the orators, preachers, and poets denied the American people the credit for their own efforts. "At no time," she commented to her sister, "did the fate of America rest upon the Breath of even a Washington, and those who assert these things, are Ignorant of the spirit of their countrymen, and whilst they strive to exalt one character degrade that of their Country."

Her best health in years and the presence of Nabby and Thomas gave Abigail great satisfaction during the winter of 1799–1800. The executive mansion became the center of social life as

Philadelphians came in droves to pay their respects before the capital was moved. Likewise, numerous representatives and senators, knowing there would be no accommodations for their families in the new federal city in the wilderness, brought their wives and daughters to Philadelphia for this session of Congress. Abigail, kept busy receiving and paying social calls and giving two or three large dinners each week, had become the First Lady in fact as well as in title. Confident of her social position, she had no hesitation in setting styles. For one, she sought by the example of her silks to make it known that muslin was not "a proper winter dress" for her republican court. Not since her days in Europe had her letters been so full of the latest fashions in clothing and hairdressing. A proper republican lady, she emphasized, should be attractively dressed and coiffed, yet modest. Even in her drawing room she spotted an occasional "outrage upon all decency" by women who displayed "the rich luxuriance of natur's Charms, at the hazard and expence of sporting with all claim to Chaste appearance."

Tommy turned into a dance one of the last social events in the Philadelphia executive mansion, a dinner for twenty-eight of his young friends. Before they left the table he asked his mother in a whisper if she had objections. "None in the world, provided it comes thus accidental," she quietly replied. From eight until twelve they danced, with the First Lady staying until the end, though the President retired after an hour. "Several of the company declared that they should always remember the Evening as one of the pleasentesst of their lives."

In his mid-sixties, with weak eyes and painful teeth, and with full knowledge of the burdens of the presidency, the longing of John Adams for retirement nearly overbalanced his lifelong quest for fame. But his wife's good health and enjoyment of her position as First Lady likely tipped the scales in favor of a decision to stand for reelection in 1800. In February Abigail wrote, "if his country calls him to continue longer in Her Service, I doubt not that he will be obedient to her voice, in which case I certainly should consider it my duty to accompany him."

The Hamiltonians desperately sought to replace Adams. To their dismay, his popularity in New England and majority support among party members in Congress, together with the lack of an attractive alternate candidate, left them with no choice. In May 1800 the President demonstrated his independence of Hamilton by removing Secretary of State Pickering and Secretary of War James McHenry. Already in April, though,

Aaron Burr had shattered any hope of an Adams-Jefferson coalition against the extreme Federalists. That crafty politician had outmaneuvered Hamilton in elections to the New York legislature and thereby ensured the state's electoral vote to the Republicans. With Jefferson and Burr as its candidates, that party sensed victory. Hamilton and his supporters hardly knew whether they were more opposed to Adams or Jefferson. But the only strategy left to them was to support the Federalist candidates while attempting secretly to manipulate the electoral college to give the vice presidential nominee, Charles Coatsworth Pinckney of South Carolina, more votes than Adams.

By the middle of May, Abigail understood the odds against her husband's reelection. A change in the presidency is "not improbable," she notified her son in Europe. She steeled herself to accept the verdict philosophically: "If the people judge that a change in the chief Majestracy of the Nation is for its peace, safety and happiness, they will no doubt make it." Like John, she felt the attractions of retirement to Quincy, though she worried more than he over their financial future. Her confidence that his decision for peace had been right, indeed essential to the nation's welfare, never wavered; and she stood with him in believing that, whatever the outcome of the election, history would vindicate the wisdom of his administration.

On May 19, 1800, Abigail set out for Quincy, leaving the President to follow after he had completed an inspection of the new capital at Washington. She stopped to see Nabby at Colonel Smith's camp in New Jersey, where his regiment was due to be disbanded. General Hamilton arrived at the same time for a final review of the troops. The colonel's men put on a smart show for the First Lady and the general. She jokingly informed John that during the review she had, as the opposition press had often charged, acted as the President's proxy. Here and along her homeward journey she listened to reports that Hamilton was visiting all the camps, even those in New England, with the message that Adams had disbanded the army but Pinckney would raise it again. There no longer existed any doubt in her mind that "this intriguer" sought to place Pinckney in the President's chair as his puppet while he ruled the nation at the head of the army.

A stop in New York City to see Charles depressed Abigail's spirits much more than rumors of Hamilton's scheming. Charles seemed glad to see her, yet ashamed, and talked incessantly in an effort to hide his condition. His mother's loving eyes searched vainly for some "hope of change." Instead, she saw that "vice and destruction have swallowd him up." "All is lost—poor, poor, unhappy, wretched man." Sally took their baby and went to her mother's, while Abigail assumed responsibility for Susan, the older child. Only "God knows what is to become of him," Abigail lamented to his older brother.

Weary and ill, she reached home; but she revived soon after John returned on July 3 with encouraging news. The warm reception he had received along his route from Washington north had led him to think that the common citizens— the backbone of the nation—were responding favorably to his patriotic appeal for a continuation of the leadership that had preserved the independence of the republic from 1776 to the present.

Abigail was sick of elections that gave rise to the basest political obscenities. The old charge of monarchy had been raised against the President. Some gullible people even believed that only the fervent pleas of Washington had stopped Adams from marrying his son to the daughter of George III in a scheme to found a new dynasty that would rule over both England and America. The Hamiltonians as well as the Republicans asserted that the President, whatever his past contributions, was now in his dotage. In October Hamilton's pamphlet attacking Adams reached the press. Thereafter the Federalists openly slashed at each other's throats. Unprotected by the Sedition Act, Jefferson fared far worse. The Federalist press repeatedly charged him with propagating atheism and planning to turn the United States over to Napoleon. Abigail resented such attacks on the man whose integrity and patriotism she still respected even while distrusting his religion, politics, and party. If a Republican was to be President, she much preferred Jefferson to any other. But she had come to wonder how many more such elections the country could withstand without breaking apart, or at least sinking into complete political degeneracy. "Calumny and falshood stop at nothing. Verily a lyeing spirit hath gone forth." She not only approved of the few sensational prosecutions of Republican editors under the Sedition Act but thought some Federalists should be similarly charged.

John had brought glowing reports of the new capital being constructed in the wilderness of Washington, but Abigail did not expect to live there unless he received a second term. However, if she was to occupy the President's House—not yet called the White House—she wanted it furnished in a manner proper for the head of a nation, even if much of the furniture had to come from Europe. Since only John would reside there during the winter, he could make do with the old furnishings moved from the executive mansion in Philadelphia, but in time the President's House must reflect the high position of its occupant.

When John prepared to leave for Washington in October, he insisted that Abigail go with him. He could not stand the thought of leaving her alone through another New England winter and argued that the warmer southern climate would be good for her health. Grumbling a bit at his sudden change of mind, she agreed to follow him soon. Sickness among relatives delayed her departure until the end of October.

On his way south the father passed through New York City without seeing the prodigal son he had renounced. Not so the mother. She found Charles, suddenly taken ill, lying "upon a Bed of sickness, destitute of a home," and living on the charity of a friend. The physicians gave no hope of recovery. Abigail went on her way knowing that "a distressing cough, an affliction of the liver, and a dropsy will soon terminate a Life, which might have been made valuable to himself and others." She had seen Charles for the last time. He died three weeks later, with only his wife and sister at the bedside. The mother took a little comfort in the thought that "he was no mans Enemy but his own." As time went by she came to believe that, given his condition, death had been "a dispensation of Heaven in Mercy to his near connections."

Abigail entered Washington on November 16, a day late from getting lost in the woods on the way from Baltimore. She discovered the new capital to be remarkable only for its perspective. In this "beautifull spot by nature," half-finished, widely scattered government buildings stood surrounded by tree stumps and connected by dirt roads which rain instantly turned into quagmires. The President's House was "upon a grand and superb scale," and Abigail knew from experience it would require at least thirty servants. Such a "great castle" was "very well proportioned to the President's salary," she sarcastically commented. Not a single room had been finished. Still damp plaster walls chilled any room without a fire, but no provision had been made to supply the President regularly with firewood. The main stairways to the second floor would not be erected for months. Abigail grew daily more irritated at the lack of bells to summon the thirteen servants with whom she tried to get by. Despite all, she experienced a sense of destiny, even as she hung clothes to dry in the "great unfinished audience-room." "This House," she wrote her sister, "is built for ages to come."

She soon knew that she would not spend the next four years in it. Federalist hopes died when South Carolina deserted its native son Pinckney for the Republicans. The official vote, opened in

February, gave Jefferson and Burr seventy-three each and Adams sixty-five, one more than Pinckney. John Adams had done remarkably well. In spite of resistance to taxation and a standing army, the Alien and Sedition Acts, and the split in the Federalist Party, a shift of a few votes would have returned him to office in a year when congressional candidates of his party fared poorly.

At the same time that Abigail learned of his defeat she also received news of his great victory in foreign policy. The commissioners had negotiated a treaty settling the major differences with France. Arriving too late to influence the election, the treaty nonetheless confirmed in the minds of John and Abigail the success of his administration. That consolation, though, could not balance for the time being the feeling of being turned out by an ungrateful country; and grief over a son dying in disgrace added to their dejection.

Even so, there was little bitterness in Abigail except against Hamilton and Burr, to whose intrigues she attributed the fall of the Federalists. She accepted the election results with more resignation than disappointment. There were "few regrets" because at her age and with her poor health she would be happier living at Quincy in modest circumstances. "If I did not rise with dignity," she wrote Tommy, "I can at least fall with ease, which is the more difficult task." Feeling no resentment against Jefferson, she hoped his administration would be "as productive of the peace, happiness, and prosperity of the nation as the two former ones."

Abigail wanted to leave for Quincy as soon as possible. As a result, she spent only three months in the new capital. Her short stay in the South proved sufficient to strengthen her opinion of the superiority of New England society. For the first time she lived in a society where slaves performed all menial labor. To her eyes, "the effects of slavery" were "visible everywhere." One of their "hardy N England men" could do the work of six "half fed," half-naked slaves. No wonder a capital city built by slave labor was far behind schedule! And slavery was equally demoralizing for non-blacks, from the idle slave owners to the poor whites, whom she found to be "a grade below the negroes in point of intelligence, and ten below them in point of civility." The discovery of the extent to which the "true Republicanism" of southerners like Jefferson rested on chattel slavery came as a shock to this daughter of New England, where the ideology of freedom employed against Great Britain had also destroyed the institution of human bondage.

The week before Christmas Abigail accepted Martha Washington's invitation to visit Mount

Vernon. Here again she marked the contrast between New England and Virginia. This decaying
plantation with its three hundred slaves seemed
a less appropriate home for the President of a
free republic than the Quincy "Farm House."
Nor was it as grand as she had heard. She came
away proud that she would not exchange homes
with the great Washington, for hers had "a
handsomer front" and its "larger rooms" were
"better furnished." The thought made retirement a little more attractive.

Early in January 1801, Jefferson accepted an
invitation to dine with the Adamses. As always,
Abigail went in to dinner on his arm. Afterwards
she thought their conversation worthy of putting
on paper because it revealed how little he knew
of the men of his party and their plans for the
nation. To her amazement she had to introduce
Jefferson to the dinner guests who were members of his own party. "I do not know one in
twenty," he admitted, after she had told him that
she knew the members of both houses of Congress, except for "a few violent" Democrats who
had refused her dinner invitations. She then used
an anecdote to preach him a little sermon on
caution over what these people he did not know
might do in the new government; "at this he
laught out, and here ended the conversation."
The election had not lessened the pleasure these

two found in each other's company. Abigail Adams still loved Thomas Jefferson's mind and spirit as much as she feared his political naïveté and religious pragmatism.

Burr's refusal to step aside for Jefferson illustrated perfectly Abigail's distrust of partisan politics. She assumed the Virginian must be the eventual choice because "neither party can tolerate Burr." Yet the potential of a deal in the House of Representatives made her shudder. "The Halcion days of America are already past," she pointed out to Uncle Tufts. Naturally, "in the present critical state of the country," she approved of John's filling as many federal offices as possible with able men. In the most famous of these "midnight appointments," John Marshall became Chief Justice. Among the others, Abigail took particular pleasure in the elevation of her nephew William Cranch to the circuit court of the District of Columbia, and in the appointment of John Quincy's bankrupt father-in-law as a revenue collector. Colonel Smith was provided a post in the Port of New York, and the Senate confirmed him with the usual malice. He was disappointed because he had wanted a brigadier general's commission in the regular army; but his mother-in-law, pleased that her daughter would have a means of support, lectured the colonel on the "strict and impartial discharge" of his new duties "with a prudent silence, without becoming the demagogue of any party."

Abigail prepared to leave the first week in February, before the House broke the tie in Jefferson's favor on the seventeenth. On the second he called on her to say farewell, wish her a "good journey," and offer his future services. Waiting for better weather, she finally set out on the thirteenth and slowly made her way on icy roads and across frozen streams to Quincy. John left Washington before daylight on the day of Jefferson's inauguration. A week later he joined Abigail in the house she had remodeled for their retirement. For the first time in their thirty-six years of married life, she did not have to anticipate another long separation from the husband whose quest for fame had become her own.

XII

"The Mother of Such a Son"

1801–1818

In 1800 Abigail Adams sat for a portrait by Gilbert Stuart. This talented but dilatory artist took years to finish, but he preserved the preliminary oil sketch from which he eventually painted a highly refined likeness. With photographic realism, the sketch showed the First Lady at fifty-six, in the year before her husband's retirement. Although the sharp lines of her face had been accented by marks of pain and disease as much as by the passage of time, the dominating eyes and resolute mouth of her youthful portraits remained to reflect her strength of mind and will.

Her last seventeen years severely tested this inner strength. By the definition of contemporary

society, she was old. Chronic illness shut her in
for long parts of most years and several times
laid her on what she thought was her deathbed.
Funerals for close relatives and friends provided
frequent reminders that she too approached the
grave. Her grandchildren proved as often disap-
pointing as pleasing. She endured another long
separation from John Quincy and suffered vic-
ariously through Nabby's unsuccessful struggle
against cancer. Almost as distressing, she
watched the nation forget her husband's contributions while deifying Washington. Her pride
as a New Englander received a heavy blow
when that section's opposition to the War of
1812 threatened to break up the union. Despite
it all, she remained so intellectually and spiritu-
ally strong that the last months before her ter-
minal illness were among the most gratifying of
her life.

The Adamses lived comfortably in retirement,
though entirely dependent upon their own resources. Not until the next century would a fru-
gal nation pension its former presidents. John
Adams now enjoyed the single governmental
perquisite of franking his letters. During his
many years of public service, Abigail had carefully preserved and enlarged their property and
encouraged small savings from his salary. This
was her retirement gift to him, but it was

threatened by the failure of a London bank in which John Quincy had advised his parents to invest most of their cash. They faced the threat of insolvency until the son sold enough of their landholdings to nearly equal the loss. John and Abigail lived within their income in order to remain independent. If their style did no honor to the high office he had held, it would be the country's disgrace, not theirs. They would go to their graves "certainly not in debt to the public." A month after the inauguration of Thomas Jefferson, Abigail wrote that she had taken up her duties as a "dairy-woman" and could be seen "skimming" milk "at five o'clock in the morning."

John, dividing his time between the farm and his books, enjoyed "a tranquility and a freedom from care" he had never known before. Abigail seemed more restless but consoled herself with the thought that labor in the garden would yield flowers and fruit rather than the crop of "calumny" and "ingratitude" harvested from public service. She regretted most that their children remained at a distance, John Quincy in Europe, Thomas in Philadelphia, and Nabby in New York. Only Louisa, one of the six children of Abigail's dead brother, and their granddaughter Susanna (Charles's daughter) made up the family at Peacefield, as John called his Quincy estate.

The return of John Quincy after an absence of seven years brightened the first year of retirement. His wife, Louisa Catherine, quickly became her father-in-law's favorite, but she was overawed by Abigail, a woman "equal to every occasion in life." Ill and feeling inferior because of her father's bankruptcy, Louisa Catherine did her best to fit the pattern of "an accomplished Quincy Lady," a role for which an indulgent upbringing had ill prepared her. The wife of John Quincy Adams must meet his mother's standards of republican womanhood. Mixing kindness with advice and instruction, Abigail undertook to prepare the new Mrs. Adams to be the helpmate of a man she already thought destined for greatness. She soon believed she had succeeded, though Louisa Catherine never lost her sense of inadequacy.

By the end of December 1801 John Quincy had settled his wife and baby son in Boston, where he opened a law office. His mother understood that the drudgery of making a living at the bar was "very far from being agreable" to a man experienced in international diplomacy. Yet she urged him not to repeat his father's example of sacrificing personal interest to serve a fickle and ungrateful nation. As much as she swelled with pride when she first heard him deliver a public oration, she remained adamant against his entering politics. But the New England Federalists needed his reputation and ability. They elected him to the state senate, ran him unsuccessfully for Congress, and in 1803 elevated him at age thirty-six to the United States Senate. That fall his mother sadly watched him leave for Washington. Nevertheless, his departure marked the political rebirth of Abigail Adams. This son's rising public career called her back to her duty as a republican mother. As he cast his first votes in the Senate, she wrote him with confidence: "I was sure you would as much as possible keep your mind free from party influence, and vote as your conscience aided by your judgement should dictate."

She had different concerns for her other son. Thirty in 1802, Thomas Boylston Adams was a bachelor with such an unsatisfactory law practice in Philadelphia that he talked of becoming a farmer in western New York. His parents would not hear of it. Abigail urged him to settle in Quincy and farm as much as he wanted while deciding his future. He finally agreed, but John Quincy bluntly advised that Tommy could not be happy in Quincy unless given complete independence from parental advice on his "mode of life." Happy to have a son at home, Abigail promised. Tommy arrived in December 1803 and lived with his parents until moving into a home of his own in 1810—his father's humble birthplace. With his mother's prodding and blessing, he married Ann Harrod of Haverhill, Massachusetts, in 1805. His meager income as a lawyer and judge left him often dependent on his parents and other family members as he and Ann began having children. In the years ahead Abigail would be deeply concerned about his drinking bouts, but at first his return added to her contentment.

Among other signs of her new serenity, she initiated a correspondence with President Jefferson that showed she could again view him as a person and not only as the rival who had defeated her husband. Even at the peak of political rivalry she had admitted how difficult it was to dislodge him from that "little corner" of her heart he had occupied so long. When she read in 1804 of the death of the President's daughter—that frightened little "Polly" Jefferson for whom she had cared in London—her "powerfull feelings . . . burst through the restraint" of partisanship. As a mother who had recently lost a son, she extended sympathy to a father grieving over the death of a daughter.

Jefferson replied in a long, warm letter expressing his continuing esteem for the Adamses. In attempting to explain why political differences had broken their friendship, he opened the door for Mrs. Adams to reply. She defended the "midnight appointments" to the judiciary, which Jefferson had written was the only action of John Adams that had ever given him "a moment's personal displeasure"; and she restated her position that it was no "infringment of the Liberty of the press, to punish the licentiousness of it." Their several exchanges of letters did clear the air of one grievance she held against him. He convinced her that he had not been a party to the removal of John Quincy from a minor federal office he had held briefly after returning from Europe.

John had known nothing of this correspondence. After five months Abigail put a stop to it with an appeal to posterity to "judge with more candour, and impartiality" the issues between them. At the end, she showed the letters to her husband, who merely noted that he had nothing to say about them at that time. It required eight more years for John Adams and Thomas Jefferson to renew their friendship. But eighteen months after her last letter to the President, Abigail applauded his promotion of her nephew, William Cranch, in the federal judiciary; and she began to find again a "little corner" of her heart for the Virginian she had once believed to be "one of the choice ones of the earth."

There would be no reconciliation with the chief antagonist of John Adams. After Vice President Burr ended Hamilton's life at Weehawken in 1804, John Quincy spoke for the family when he refused to attend a memorial service because he would not "join in any outward demonstration of regret" which he "could not feel at heart." Abigail could not acknowledge the merit of any man she considered an enemy of her husband: "Why deceive the public and give that which is more than due and leave nothing to bestow upon fairer and purer Characters? . . . he was the Idol of a party . . . who have injured their cause, and their Country more than Hamilton ever served it."

His death reminded Abigail and John that New York City was the source of their greatest misfortunes. Hamilton and Burr had hatched their intrigues there; Charles had lost his life in its fleshpots; and it was the home of Colonel Smith, whose troubles were far from over. In 1805 the colonel became ensnared in the scheme of his "intimate friend" of many years, Francisco de Miranda, to launch a filibustering expedition against Venezuela as the first blow for the liberation of Spain's South American colonies. Believing Miranda's assurances that he had received the tacit approval of the American government, Smith took a leading part in fitting out a ship and recruiting men. His oldest son, William Steuben Smith, enlisted with his mother's blessing but without a hint to the grandparents. Soon after this comic-opera expedition sailed in February 1806, the Spanish ambassador got wind of its purpose and pressed President Jefferson into disowning it. Colonel Smith, the most conspicuous abettor of Miranda, was dismissed from his position as surveyor of the port, indicted for conspiracy, and arrested. After a well-publicized trial in the summer, a sympathetic New York jury took only two hours to acquit him. But he was left unemployed and with no hope of another federal position.

Abigail and John were so dismayed at their son-in-law's "credulity" that they did not blame Jefferson for removing him from office. They feared most for the life of their grandson, especially following reports that some of Miranda's men had been captured by the Spanish. After the expedition had ended in total failure, William made his way safely home, only to find his father ruined. Colonel Smith had no better alternative than to send his family to Quincy while he built a house for them on his brother's land in the New York wilderness south of Lake Oneida. Late in 1807 he moved his wife and daughter to this isolated spot. As always, Nabby followed her husband with resignation and forced cheerfulness. In Abigail's eyes, though, her only daughter, through no fault of her own, had been sentenced to a "seclusion from the world" that deprived her of every "social enjoyment."

In November 1807, before the Smiths left for the wilderness and Senator Adams departed for Washington, Abigail enjoyed the rare pleasure of having all her children and all but one of the grandchildren seated around her dinner table at once. They reminded her of a "live plant" with rapidly growing branches. She loved them all and had high hopes for the third generation. Yet she knew already that the family's chances for greatness in the second generation rested solely on the shoulders of her eldest son.

As Senator Adams neared forty, his mother still felt a duty to advise him and appealed to his wife to join her in improving his health and appearance. She urged Louisa Catherine never to let him go to the Senate "without a craker in his pocket," for "the space between breakfast and dinner is so long, that his stomach gets fill'd with flatulencies, and his food when he takes it neither dijests or nourishes him." Abigail admitted her thirty-year failure to instill proper habits of dress in this son, and she applauded Louisa Catherine's greater success. She reminded him that he should be grateful to have a wife take over this duty from his mother: even "the neatest Man . . . wants his wife to pull up his coller, and mind that his coat is brush'd." If Senator Adams appeared in that august body with an unshaven face or carelessly dressed, the world would "ask what kind of a Mother he had" or charge his wife with "neglegence and inattention when she is guiltless."

Upon entering the Senate, John Quincy Adams had been compelled by his experience abroad and his "sense of duty" to vote with the administration on crucial issues of foreign policy. Of all New England Federalists in Congress, he alone favored the Louisiana Purchase. In 1807 he embittered the Massachusetts Federalists even more by voting for the embargo President Jefferson had proposed as a method of retaliating against French and British attacks on American shipping. By then, Senator Adams was a Republican in all but name. His conversion became public the following year when he accepted an invitation to attend the caucus of congressional Republicans to select that party's nominees for the presidential election.

Abigail was indignant. She objected not so much to his siding with the Republicans as to the principle of a caucus, which she held to be "an infringment upon the *freedom* and *purity* of Elections" because the Constitution left the presidential electors free to exercise their best judgment. John Quincy answered with a defense of the caucus as necessary to effect "a concert of opinions." Being "merely advisory," its recommendations did not interfere with the freedom of elections. Abigail accepted his reasoning and rejoiced that she had a son who could write her, "I could wish to please my Country—I could wish to please my Parents—But my duty, I *must* do—It is a Law far above that of my mere wishes."

This republican mother had no difficulty in defending her son's politics, particularly after the Massachusetts legislature elected a partisan Federalist to succeed him. His party, she wrote, "have vilified, abused and calumniated him because he could not adopt their principles and become a party Man, because he would have an opinion of his own." By contrast the Republicans had accepted him "as he really is, a man of candid liberal mind, free from party views, of a pure heart, and unblemished Character, of distinguished tallents and integrity." Her pride knew no limit: "I consider it as a family trophy, as a coat of arms and pride myself more being the Mother of such a son, than in all the honours and titles which [a] Monarch could bestow." During the election of 1808, Abigail easily decided that Madison, the politician she had most feared in 1790, was better qualified to be President than the candidate of the party that had treated her son in such a dishonorable manner.

But she was so disgusted with elections that she favored giving the President a twelve-year term as a means of adding stability to the federal government and reducing the "warfare of Ambition and intrigue."

Senator Adams resigned before the end of his term and returned to his law practice and to the Harvard professorship he had held since 1806. His retirement from public life lasted little more than a year. In June 1809 the Senate confirmed his appointment as United States minister to Russia. He accepted without a moment's hesitation. On August 5, 1809, with his wife and baby son, he boarded a ship bound for Saint Petersburg. His parents were devastated. "The separation was like tearing me to Pieces," wrote John Adams. To Abigail at sixty-five, it seemed almost certainly a final farewell. "At the advanced years both of his Father and Myself, we can have very little expectation of meeting again upon this mortal theater." Her son, she believed, had been driven from the country by "the intolerant Spirit of party."

Within a year Mrs. Adams had recovered sufficiently from the shock of her son's departure to understand that his temporary removal from domestic politics only enhanced his reputation. She reported to him such Republican toasts given on July 4, 1810, as "J. Q. Adams, already Number'd in the list of our great and good Men." Her reservations concerning government service gave way to a belief that he was destined to serve his country "in her most essential, and important Interests, for Years yet to come." She judged him to be of presidential caliber but much preferred to see him safely seated on the Supreme Court than in the highest office, whose torments she knew too well. Such a man should not be permitted to remain for long out of a country short of capable and virtuous leaders. After John Quincy and Louisa Catherine had written of their misery in the long, frigid Russian winters and of the impossibility of living in this court on the salary Congress granted its ministers, Abigail appealed to President Madison to bring her son home.

Madison responded in 1811 by granting Adams permission to return if he desired and offering him an appointment to the Supreme Court. By then, however, John Quincy had settled his family more comfortably and saw new opportunities to serve his country at the tsar's court. Furthermore, Louisa Catherine was pregnant, and he did not want to subject her to the six-thousand-mile voyage. This decision, Abigail wrote, "cast a great damp upon my spirits." But she struggled to keep alive the hope of seeing her son again.

The year 1811 held even greater agony for Abigail Adams. In January she learned that her daughter had discovered a rapidly enlarging tumor in one breast. Nabby came in July to consult physicians in Boston, who hesitatingly pronounced it cancerous but prescribed no drastic treatment. She then turned for advice to the close friend of her parents, Dr. Benjamin Rush of Philadelphia. He urged immediate surgery as the only possibility of saving her life. Supported by family and friends, Nabby submitted to the knife. On October 8 the entire breast was removed with only opium as an anesthetic. She endured the ordeal with "calmness and fortitude," and the surgeons pronounced her cured. After a long convalescence in Quincy, she returned the following summer to her wilderness home. Throughout the next winter she suffered severe pain, diagnosed at first as rheumatism; but by spring 1813 her condition was undeniable. Elected to Congress, Colonel Smith had gone off to Washington, leaving his eighteen-year-old daughter Caroline to care for her mother. Nabby resolved to spend whatever time she had left in her parents' home. With her brother's help, Caroline took her pain-racked mother by slow stages to Quincy. She arrived late in July and was put to bed. The end came quickly, on August 15, a few days after her husband reached her bedside.

The mother had never known such sorrow, even over Charles. She tried to write John Quincy what she felt: "The wound which has lacerated my Bosom cannot be healed. The broken Heart may be bound up; and religion teach submission and silence, even under the anguish of the Heart, but it cannot cure it. The unbidden sigh will rise, and the bitter tear flow long after the Tomb is closed."

Abigail had endured this tragedy without the support of her nearby sister. In October 1811, the week after Nabby's surgery, Richard and Mary Cranch died on successive days, neither wanting to live after the other had gone. Abigail had made a small payment on the debt she owed the Cranches by organizing nursing care for them during their final days. The two older sons of John Quincy Adams, who had boarded with the Cranches while preparing for college, now went to live with their Aunt Elizabeth and attend her husband's academy. As always, Abigail's younger sister struggled to rise above the drudgery of her life. Early in 1812, with only her daughter's help, she was boarding eleven males of the academy. Soon she too was gone, dying suddenly in 1815. In some respects the brightest of the Smith sisters, Elizabeth had served as a reminder to Abigail of what her life might have been without the fortunate marriage to John Adams. Surely she understood how impossible the unusual life she had led would have been without the support of such remarkable sisters. Now that she was the only surviving child of her parents, Abigail heard a "loud call . . . to live in a habitual preparation for a summons to depart." But the hope of once more embracing her oldest son remained a vital force to keep her alive.

The outbreak of war between the United States and that "old Sorcress" England, together with the almost simultaneous invasion of Russia by Napoleon, had dimmed that hope. But worry over her son's perilous position did not deter Mrs. Adams from supporting her country. She wrote in 1813, "I am one of those who believe in the Righteousness and justice of the present War with Great Britain." Just as the Revolution had been necessary to obtain independence, the new war was essential to preserve it. By opposing the war, even to the point of advocating secession, New England's extreme Federalists had degraded their section, she lamented. In a letter to John Quincy she wrote words that could almost have come from Jefferson's pen: "Where is the true Native American Spirit? it dwells in the Breasts of our uncorrupted Natives, in our Yeomanry, in our sailors, and in our few remaining old patriots. Where dwells British influence? in our Banks, in our Warehouses, in our Commerce." Among other demonstrations of loyalty, she refused to listen to preachers who thundered against "Mr. Madison's War." She took great pride in the victories of United States naval vessels under the command of officers commissioned during the administration of President Adams, "The Father of the American Navy."

Most important for Abigail Adams, the War of 1812 was a conflict her son helped to end. Just as his father had been one of the commissioners who negotiated an end to the War for Independence, John Quincy Adams was ordered to join the peace commission for the present war. Since going abroad, he had made his mother his most frequent correspondent, and his letters had kept her fully informed on European developments. In typical fashion, a few hours after he had signed the "Peace of Christmas Eve" at Ghent, Belgium, he wrote the happy news to his mother before anyone else. By mid-February 1815, she was singing the praises of General Andrew Jackson for his victory at New Orleans—a battle fought after the peace had been concluded—and explaining to friends and neighbors why her son had put his signature to a treaty that did little except end the war.

Peace did not bring John Quincy home. Again duplicating his father's career, early in 1815 he was appointed minister to Great Britain. Abigail found this disappointment the most poignant yet, and more so during a near-fatal illness in the first months of 1816. Still, she enjoyed comparing the England she had known with that described in the letters of John Quincy and Louisa Catherine. "What delight We garrulous old people take in living over again, in our offspring," she acknowledged. This joy helped to restore her in the summer to what her husband described as "her characteristic Vivacity, Activity, Will, Sense and benevolence."

The hour she lived for finally came. In March 1817 John Quincy Adams was appointed Secretary of State, and he and his family reached Quincy on August 18, the happiest day in Abigail's old age. Their reunion of barely three weeks before he left for Washington stimulated a last rejuvenation in this woman who felt her age. Louisa Catherine's journal-like letters from the capital gave Abigail Adams a final year of republican motherhood. In answering one of them, she advised her daughter-in-law to expect envy in their political associates because "an Heir apparent is always envied."

Abigail would not live to see this "Heir apparent" continue along his father's path to become a one-term President. But she thought she saw her political faith vindicated during the early years of President Monroe's administration. The temporary absence of contending parties at the national level in this Era of Good Feelings renewed her confidence that the best and brightest men of both parties would unite to eliminate the partisanship that she believed had nearly destroyed the infant republic. Since 1812 she had watched with satisfaction the reconciliation of her husband and Jefferson. In one of her last letters to the Virginian she expressed the regret that she was too old to do more than reflect upon past pleasures, "amongst which, and not the least is my early acquaintance with, and the continued Friendship of the phylosopher of Monticello."

She saw hope also in the Unitarian movement now spreading through many of the churches in the Boston area. Opposed to creeds and disputes over them, she nevertheless welcomed the liberalization of Christianity as the best means of teaching the simple faith that she freely confessed. Nothing could convince her that "three is one, and one three." There was only one God, and he had sent Jesus Christ into the world to set an example of the life one must strive to lead, as far as is humanly possible, to gain "future happiness in the world to come." She could never be a narrow sectarian: "We are assured that those who fear God and work righteousness shall be accepted of him, and that I presume of what ever sect, or persuasion." Or, as she also wrote, "When will Mankind be convinced that true Religion is from the Heart, between Man and his creator, and not the imposition of Man or creeds and tests?" For her there existed a close relationship between the religious and political strength of the republic, for "that cannot be politically right which is morally wrong." Unitarianism, with its stress upon the divine being's "visible qualities such as wisdom, power, and goodness," could better impress that connection upon the minds of citizens than the narrow creeds of dogmatic churches.

Old age was a time for reconciliation with Mercy Otis Warren, whose writings on the American Revolution had widened the gulf separating the two families who had been close in Revolutionary days. And there was a measure of forgiveness for Colonel Smith. His exemplary conduct in the last years before his death in 1816 renewed Abigail's early opinion that he had been a "Brave officer" of "a Noble and generous Spirit, a tender heart, and kind affections," whose misfortunes had resulted from gullibility rather than more serious defects of character. Abigail was noticeably more tolerant of the shortcomings of the colonel's eldest son, William Steuben Smith, than was his Uncle John Quincy, whom William served as secretary in Russia.

Similarly, she involved herself in the successes and failures of her adult grandchildren with a loving patience that endeared her to them.

Living into the nineteenth century strengthened Abigail's view of the separate but reciprocal roles of the sexes. If she had ever harbored desires to encroach on the male prerogative, they were gone now. In a letter of 1809 to her sister Elizabeth she spoke plainly: "No man ever prospered in the world without the consent and cooperation of his wife. It behoves us . . . to give our daughters and granddaughters . . . such an education as shall qualify them for the useful and domestic duties of life. . . . I consider it as an indispensable requisite, that every American wife should herself know how to order and regulate her family; how to govern her domestics, and train up her children. For this purpose, the all-wise Creator made woman an help-meet for man, and she who fails in these duties does not answer the end of her creation."

As completely as she believed that "nature has assigned to each sex their particular duties and sphere of action," Abigail never ceased to insist on the equal importance of the male and female roles or on the right of a woman to judge how well her husband and sons met their responsibilities. Domestic duties might prevent most women from becoming truly learned, but the proper education of the more capable daughters was as essential as college for the brightest sons. "It is very certain," she wrote, "that a well-informed woman, conscious of her nature and dignity, is more capable of performing the relative duties of life, and of engaging and retaining the affections of a man of understanding, than one whose intellectual endowments rise not above the common level." Few men could be better than the wives they married. If republican society was to achieve its high promise, the ablest women must be trained for and gladly assume their responsibility.

Abigail's satisfaction with her own marriage undoubtedly added conviction to her view. As her fiftieth wedding anniversary neared, she reflected that she had "gone through a long Life with as few Rubs of a matrim[oni]al nature" as any woman could expect. She and John had not always agreed. In some cases she had insisted on getting her own way and in others had yielded silently. But her final assessment was clear: "Yet after half a century, I can say, my first choice would be the same if I again had youth, and opportunity to make it." By contrast, she saw around her women whose fate had been sealed in less fortunate and sometimes tragic marriages. The lesson was obvious: no woman should enter into marriage lightly. She advised her granddaughters and nieces "to look out Well. The die once cast, there is no retreat untill death."

Notwithstanding her recurrent illnesses, Abigail's mind remained clear and vigorous into her seventies. She eagerly read and passed judgment on the latest literature. Sir Walter Scott she preferred to Lord Byron, but she judged them both inferior to her "sterling" favorites, Milton, Pope, and Thomson. She read and praised Madame de Staël's *On Germany* and took great interest in the visit of John Quincy to that notorious author in France. One of her last letters, in August 1818, reported to Louisa Catherine that she was reading a biography of Andrew Jackson and had come to admire the general as his character was described in this volume. Death spared her the distasteful necessity of forming a lower opinion of the military hero who became her son's political rival and the symbol of much that she detested in American life.

John Quincy brought his family for a short visit in September and left for Washington in early October. Abigail contracted typhus fever soon thereafter. For two weeks she seemed in little danger, but then sank rapidly and died on October 28, 1818, less than a month before her seventy-fourth birthday. Though now eighty-three, John insisted on walking in the funeral procession as a last tribute to his "fellow Labourer" of fifty-four years. They endured another of their many separations until his death eight years later on the fiftieth anniversary of the Declaration of Independence. Had she lived, Abigail would have best understood how appropriate it was for Jefferson to die on that same Fourth of July, a few hours before John Adams.

* * *

The life of Abigail Adams was unlike that of contemporary American women. Most were poor and burdened with monotonous domestic labor; she always enjoyed relative affluence and never lived a day unattended by servants. Most had little or no educational opportunity; she was surrounded by books from the cradle to the grave. Most had no choice but to marry men who accepted female inferiority; she married a man who respected her intellect and valued her counsel. Most spent their lives in one location or in a succession of provincial communities; she lived in the leading metropolises of the western world. Most had little opportunity to acquire political knowledge; she conversed with statesmen in Europe and the United States and wrote long letters of political commentary. Few if any of her countrywomen matched her experience.

Despite her uniqueness—or perhaps because of it—Abigail Adams developed a keen sensibility to the liabilities of being born female in a paternalistic society. Her personal effort to overcome

or adjust to these handicaps provided a conspicuous illustration of the plight of all American
women. She denounced the potential for tyranny
in the legal subjection of wives to husbands, and
she believed a woman should be free to make a
prudent choice of a mate and to limit the number
of children she bore. Refusing to accept the inferiority of the female intellect, she added her influence to the growing demand for the education of
girls. Her acceptance of the doctrine of separate
spheres for men and women fixed the boundaries
of her feminism. But within these limits she
maintained that the private political role of
women in a republic was fully as important as
the public one of the male.

That role, which she exemplified and advocated
for other women of her class, can be summarized
as republican womanhood. Virtue for females
was no longer to be confined to chastity, prudence, and charity. It had expanded to include the
obligation, through courtship, marriage, and
motherhood, to send into society husbands
and sons dedicated to the male virtues of self-sac-
rificial public service and incorruptible patriotism. Republican womanhood provided for the
first time a political function for women, by
which private virtue became a public benefit.
"Public Virtue is the only Foundation of Re-
publics," wrote John Adams, but it "cannot exist

in a Nation without private" virtue. As a lonely wife seeing her husband sail for France in 1778, Abigail could take "satisfaction in the Consciousness of having discharged my duty to the public" by not insisting that he stay home to care for her and the children. By the time she became First Lady, she had lost confidence that America could escape the corruptions of mother England. Thus it became even more important for virtuous women to fulfill their duty to the state. Her advocacy of republican motherhood provided a strong argument for the education of women, but it confined most women to the home and did not weaken the doctrine of coverture for which she had pleaded in 1776. Literacy in itself without legal changes was not an argument for the equality of men and women. Still, the better-educated generations of her granddaughters and great-granddaughters would take up and expand the issues she had made clear in her "Remember the Ladies" letter to a husband engaged in nation-building. She too believed she had taken a part in the building of the American nation.

It was fitting that the son in whom she took so much pride should pass the ultimate judgment on Abigail Adams. In commenting to his brother on their mother's death, John Quincy Adams wrote, "Her life gave the lie to every libel on her sex that was ever written."

A Note on the Sources

This book is based largely on the correspondence of Abigail Adams and her family. Most of these letters are in the Adams Papers, the collection of family manuscripts now located at the Massachusetts Historical Society. All of the Adams Papers are available in a microfilm edition of 608 reels (Boston: Massachusetts Historical Society, 1954–59). Reels 97, 197, 343–445 contain the correspondence of Mrs. Adams and additional material relating to her, and other reels provide information on selected topics. The papers of the Adams family from all sources are receiving definitive publication by the Massachusetts Historical Society in a project that promises to outlast several generations of editors. These volumes are presently available, all published by the Harvard University Press: *Adams Family Correspondence,* vols. 1–6

(1963–93); *Papers of John Adams,* vols. 1–10 (1977–96); *Diary and Autobiography of John Adams,* 4 vols. (1961); *Diary of John Quincy Adams,* vols. 1–2 (1981); *The Earliest Diary of John Adams* (1966); *Legal Papers of John Adams,* 3 vols. (1965); *Portraits of John and Abigail Adams* (1967). Not part of the Adams Papers but published under the same auspices is *The Book of Abigail and John: Selected Letters of the Adams Family, 1762–1784* (1975).

Outside the Adams Papers, the Massachusetts Historical Society has approximately 130 letters of Mrs. Adams. Twelve of these for 1808 and 1811 were published in the society's *Proceedings* 66 (Oct. 1936–May 1941), 126–153, ed. Allyn B. Forbes; and others in *Warren-Adams Letters,* 2 vols. (1917, 1925), Mass. Hist. Soc. *Collections,* vols. 72, 73. The Shaw Family Papers at the Library of Congress include 112 letters written by Mrs. Adams to her sister, Elizabeth Shaw-Peabody, and to other members of the Shaw family. The American Antiquarian Society has approximately 250 letters to the other sister, Mary Cranch, of which 141 were published in *New Letters of Abigail Adams, 1788–1801,* ed. Stewart Mitchell (Boston: Houghton Mifflin Co., 1947). The Boston Public Library possesses 27 letters, and the Historical Society of Pennsylvania has a smaller collection. The Johnson Family Papers, given to the Cornell University Library in 1996, have 17 letters written in her later years to her daughter-in-law and to her grandaughter. Other letters are widely scattered throughout many institutions.

Until the opening of the Adams Papers, most readers had known Abigail Adams through the volumes edited by her grandson, Charles Francis Adams. In 1840 he published *Letters of Mrs. Adams, the Wife of John Adams. With an Introductory Memoir*. This work proved so popular that new and enlarged editions appeared in 1840, 1841, and 1848. He also brought out a centennial volume of *Familiar Letters of John Adams and His Wife Abigail Adams, during the Revolution* (1876); which quickly became an American classic. Three other collections by the same editor are still useful: *Letters of John Adams, Addressed to his Wife*, 2 vols. (1841); *The Works of John Adams*, 10 vols. (1850–56); and *Memoirs of John Quincy Adams, Comprising Portions of His Diary from 1795–1848*, 12 vols. (1874–77).

The granddaughter of Abigail Adams, Caroline Smith de Windt, published the *Journal and Correspondence of Miss Adams, Daughter of John Adams*, 2 vols. (1841, 1842), which contains a few family letters not found elsewhere.

The Adams-Jefferson Letters: The Complete Correspondence Between Thomas Jefferson and Abigail and John Adams, ed. Lester J. Cappon, 2 vols. (Chapel Hill: University of North Carolina Press, for the Institute of Early American History and Culture, Williamsburg, 1959), conveniently assembles their scattered letters. A highly selective but useful sample of family correspondence is in *Writings of John Quincy Adams,* ed. Worthington Chauncey Ford, 7 vols. (1913–17). Among the other family manuscripts, the diaries of William Smith (Abigail's father), Dr. Cotton Tufts (her uncle), and Elizabeth Cranch (her niece), all at the Mass. Hist. Soc., are especially valuable. The diaries of Smith and Tufts were partially published in the society's *Proceedings* 42 (1908–09), 444–478. Portions of the Cranch diary are in the *Essex Institute Historical Collections* 79 (1943), 1–36.

Abigail Adams always lamented that she had been denied the education necessary to bring her spelling, punctuation, grammar, and syntax up to the literary standards of her day. Charles Francis Adams lovingly corrected these faults in his grandmother's letters and suppressed some passages he considered unsuitable for publication. Modern editors have also puzzled over how to transcribe her script. Thus the reader will note considerable variation in style among the quotations from her letters. In this book, quotations are taken from a modern scholarly edition where available; but if not, from the manuscripts; or, as a last resort, from one of the family editors. However, in a few cases the polished version of Charles Francis Adams has been used to retain the flavor of a passage long familiar to the public, provided it contains no serious distortion of the original. In transcribing from the manuscript letters, the original is followed, with these exceptions: each sentence is begun with a capital letter; an apostrophe is added to indicate the elision of a final vowel; commas are added in a series when necessary for clarity; the ampersand is written out, and a few untypical spelling errors are silently corrected when essential for intelligibility. Since it is often impossible to distinguish between her capital and lower case letters, her common practice was used as a guide.

The 1980 edition of this book was the first biography of Abigail Adams since the Adams manuscripts were opened to scholars. Since then two fuller volumes have appeared: Phyllis Lee Levin, *Abigail Adams* (New York: St. Martin's Press, 1987); and Lynne Withey, *Dearest Friend: A Life of Abigail Adams* (New York: Free Press, 1981). Both closely tie their subject's life to the political careers of her husband and of her famous son. By contrast, Edith B. Gelles attempts in two volumes, through a topical approach, to produce a portrait of "a woman, not of her men": *Portia: the World of Abigail Adams* (Bloomington: Indiana University Press, 1992) and *First Thoughts: Life and Letters of Abigail Adams* (New York: Twayne Publishers, 1998). For a short introduction to Abigail Adams nothing surpasses L. H. Butterfield's incisive sketch in *Notable American Women, 1607–1950: A Biographical Dictionary,* eds. Edward T. and Janet W. James, 3 vols. (Cambridge, Mass.: Harvard University Press, 1971).

With an extensive mastery of all the Adams Papers, Paul C. Nagel has published three volumes that deal in part with Abigail Adams: *The Adams Women: Abigail and Louisa Adams, their Sisters and Daughters* (New York: Oxford University Press, 1987); *Descent from Glory: Four Generations of the John Adams Family* (New York: Oxford University Press, 1983); and *John Quincy Adams: A Public Life, a Private Life* (New York: Alfred A. Knopf, 1997). In all three volumes, Nagel viewed Abigail harshly as an aggressive, domineering person who was "a calamity of a mother." Nagel appears overly impressed by the views of the later generations of Adamses who sometimes found it difficult to live up to the rigorous "Adams doctrine" they

believed had been established by the first generation. He fails to judge Abigail in comparison to
other contemporary middle-class parents who
similarly sought to establish high standards for
their children but did not preserve those views in
such a mass of documentation as the Adams
manuscripts provide.

The leading biography of John Adams remains
Page Smith, *John Adams,* 2 vols. (Garden City,
N.Y.: Doubleday & Co., 1962). John Ferling,
John Adams: A Life (Knoxville: University of
Tennessee Press, 1992) is an admirable one-vol-
ume biography. In *John Adams* (New York:
Simon & Schuster, 2001), David McCullough
removes Adams from the shadows of Franklin
and Jefferson and ascribes to him an equal role
in the creation of the American Republic. Joseph
J. Ellis, *Passionate Sage: The Character and
Legacy of John Adams* (New York: W.W.
Norton, 1993) concentrates on the years after
Adams left the presidency. Essential to under-
standing the identification of Mrs. Adams with
her husband is Douglass Adair, "Fame and the
Founding Fathers," in *Fame and the Founding
Fathers,* ed. Trevor Colbourn (New York: W. W.
Norton, 1974). Walt Brown, *John Adams and
the American Press* (Jefferson, N.C.: McFarland
& Co., 1995) studies the relation of Adams to
the press during his presidential years. On John

Quincy Adams, in addition to Nagel's biography, Samuel Flagg Bemis, *John Quincy Adams and the Foundations of American Foreign Policy* (New York: Alfred A, Knopf, 1949) remains important. Jack Shepherd's *Cannibals of the Heart: A Personal Biography of Louisa Catherine and John Quincy Adams* (New York: Oxford University Press, 1983) concentrates on the relation between this husband and wife but with considerable attention to Abigail Adams. Among the other children, only the daughter has caught the fancy of biographers. *Colonel William Smith and Lady,* by Katharine Metcalf Roof (Boston: Houghton Mifflin Co., 1929), stresses the romantic aspects of their courtship and marriage, as does Lida Mayo's "Miss Adams in Love," *American Heritage* 16 (Feb. 1965), 36–39, 80–89. There are some interesting recollections of Elizabeth Shaw-Peabody and her second husband in Samuel Gilman, *Contributions to Literature* ... (Boston, 1856). Numerous male relatives and acquaintances of Mrs. Adams have had their lives brilliantly sketched by Clifford K. Shipton in the later volumes of *Sibley's Harvard Graduates.*

The rich local history of Weymouth, Braintree, and Quincy can be studied in the manuscript records of the North Parish (First Precinct) of Weymouth, 1735–1825 (microfilm at the Mass.

Hist. Soc.); *Records of the Town of Braintree, 1640–1793*, ed. Samuel A. Bates (1886); William S. Pattee, *A History of Old Braintree and Quincy* . . . (1878); Daniel Munro Wilson, *Where American Independence Began* . . . (1904); and *History of Weymouth, Massachusetts,* 4 vols. (Weymouth: Weymouth Historical Society, 1923). *A Pride of Quincys* (Boston: Mass. Hist. Soc., 1969) summarizes and illustrates the Quincy family history. The maternal grandfather of Mrs. Adams received his due in Daniel Munro Wilson's *John Quincy* . . . (Boston, 1909). Josiah Quincy, *Figures of the Past* (Boston, 1926), adds interesting glimpses of some members of the family.

Howard C. Rice, Jr.'s *Thomas Jefferson's Paris* (Princeton: Princeton University Press, 1976) and his *The Adams Family in Auteuil, 1784–1785* (Boston: Mass. Hist. Soc., 1956) illuminate the residence of the Adamses in that city; as does Claude-Anne Lopez, *Mon Cher Papa, Franklin and the Ladies of Paris* (New Haven: Yale University Press, 1966). Ralph Ketcham calls attention to the mutual attraction between Jefferson and Mrs. Adams in "The Puritan Ethic in the Revolutionary Era: Abigail Adams and Thomas Jefferson," in *"Remember the Ladies": New Perspectives on Women in American History,* ed. Carol V. R. George (Syracuse:

Syracuse University Press, 1975), 49–65. Joseph
J. Ellis, *American Sphinx: The Character of
Thomas Jefferson* (New York: Alfred A. Knopf,
1998) contains much material on the relations of
Jefferson with the Adamses. Gary B. Nash
describes the intellectual climate in which
Abigail Adams turned against French influence
in "The American Clergy and the French
Revolution," *William and Mary Quarterly* 22
(July 1965), 392–412. Her admiration for the
English female historian is understandable after
reading Lucy Martin Donnelly, "The Celebrated
Mrs. Macaulay," *William and Mary Quarterly* 6
(April 1949), 173–207. John Duffy furnishes
much of the background required to compre-
hend her medical experience in *Epidemics in
Colonial America* (Baton Rouge: Louisiana State
University Press, 1953), and in the first chapters
of *The Healers: The Rise of the Medical
Establishment* (New York: McGraw-Hill, 1976).
The significance of the childbirth experience is
explored in Catherine M. Scholten, "'On the
Importance of the Obstetric Art': Changing
Customs of Childbirth in America, 1760–1825,"
William and Mary Quarterly 34 (July 1977),
426–445.

The influence of Pope on Mrs. Adams can be
gleaned from the commentary she studied: Joseph
Warton, *An Essay on the Genius and Writings of*

Pope, 2 vols. (New York: Garland Publishing Co., 1970; reprinted from the 4th ed., London, 1782). The following modern studies of her favorite authors are helpful: Ralph Cohen, *The Unfolding of the Seasons* (Baltimore: Johns Hopkins University Press, 1970); Cynthia Griffin Wolff, *Samuel Richardson and the Eighteenth-Century Puritan Character* (Hamden, Conn.: Archon Books, 1972); and *Samuel Richardson, A Collection of Critical Essays,* ed. John Carroll (Englewood Cliffs, N.J.: Prentice-Hall, 1969). Zoltan Haraszti's analysis of the marginalia in the books in the Adams library (*John Adams & the Prophets of Progress* [Cambridge, Mass.: Harvard University Press, 1952]) reveals much of the intellectual climate of the Adams family circle. That library is catalogued in *Catalogue of the John Adams Library in the Public Library of the City of Boston* (Boston, 1917). The close relationship of the Adamses with the physician-philosopher Benjamin Rush can be studied from *Letters of Benjamin Rush,* ed. L. H. Butterfield, 2 vols. (Princeton: Princeton University Press, 1951); *The Autobiography of Benjamin Rush,* ed. George W. Corner (Princeton: Princeton University Press, 1948); and *Old Family Letters . . . ,* ed. Alexander Biddle (1892). Some of the flavor of the political and social life in the capitals of the infant republic is captured in *Journal of William Maclay,* ed.

Edgar S. Maclay (1890); and Bradford Perkins, "A Diplomat's Wife in Philadelphia: Letters of Henrietta Liston, 1796–1800," *William and Mary Quarterly* 11 (Oct. 1954), 592–632.

Among the most significant books on Revolutionary women are Mary Beth Norton, *Liberty's Daughters: The Revolutionary Experience of American Women, 1750–1800* (Ithaca: Cornell University Press, 1980); Linda Kerber, *Women of the Republic: Intellect and Ideology in Revolutionary America* (Chapel Hill: University of North Carolina Press, 1980); Nancy F. Cott, *The Bonds of Womanhood: "Woman's Sphere" in New England, 1780–1835* (New Haven: Yale University Press, 1977); and Linda Grant DePauw and Conover Hunt, *"Remember the Ladies": Women in America, 1780–1815* (New York: Viking Press, 1976). These volumes examine the experiences of women and what they wrote about themselves rather than the writings of others about them. Some of Linda Kerber's essays extend this method of historical inquiry in *Toward an Intellectual History of Women* (Chapel Hill: University of North Carolina Press, 1997). Joan R. Gunderson in *To Be Useful to the World: Women in Revolutionary America* (New York: Twayne Publishers, 1996) uses case histories to extend her study of Revolutionary women over three decades. Cathy N. Davidson in *Revolution and the Word: The Rise of the Novel in America* (New York: Oxford University Press, 1986) describes and interprets the revolution in fictional reading for women underway between 1789 and 1820. Rosemarie Zagarri, *A Woman's Dilemma: Mercy Otis Warren and the American Revolution* (Wheeling, IL: Harlan Davidson, 1995) provides important perspective on the relation of the Adamses to the Warrens. W. J. Rorabaugh, *The Alcoholic Republic: An American Tradition* (New York: Oxford University Press, 1979) probes the problem with alcohol faced by men of Abigail's generation. On childbirth see Catherine M. Scholten, *Childbearing in American Society, 1650–1850* (New York: New York University Press, 1985).

Several articles offer perspective on the experiences of Abigail Adams: Joan Hoff-Wilson, "The Illusion of Change: Women and the American Revolution" in *The American Revolution: Explorations in the History of American Radicalism*, ed. Alfred F. Young (DeKalb, IL: Northern Illinois University Press, 1976), 383–445; Linda Grant Depauw, "The American Revolution and the Rights of Women: The Feminist Theory of Abigail Adams" in *The Legacy of the American Revolution*, ed. Larry R.

Gerlach, et al. (Logan, Utah: Utah State University Press, 1978); Ruth H. Bloch, "The Gendered Meaning of Virtue in Revolutionary America," *Signs* XIII (1987), 39–58; "American Feminine Ideals in Transition: The Rise of the Moral Mother, 1785–1815," *Feminist Studies* 42 (1978), 101–126; Jan Lewis, "The Republican Wife: Virtue and Seduction in the Early Republic," *William and Mary Quarterly,* 3rd series, XLIV (1987), 689–721; and Joan R. Gunderson, "Independence, Citizenship, and the American Revolution," *Signs* XIII (1987), 59–77.

But after reading everything else, it is essential to return to the letters of Abigail Adams, in which there remains much more than any of her biographers have extracted.

Acknowledgments

This book would have been impossible without the cooperation of the institutions that have collected, preserved, and in some cases published the manuscripts of the Adams family. I am indebted to the Massachusetts Historical Society for permission to quote from the microfilm edition of the Adams Papers and from other manuscript collections; to the Harvard University Press for permission to quote from the *Adams Family Correspondence,* from the *Diary and Autobiography of John Adams,* from *The Book of Abigail and John,* from the *Diary of John Quincy Adams,* and from the *Papers of John Adams;* to Thomas B. Adams for permission to quote from the Shaw Papers; to the American Antiquarian Society, Worcester, Massachusetts, for permission to quote from the Abigail Adams Letters, 1784–1816; to The University of North

Carolina Press for permission to quote from *The Adams-Jefferson Letters: The Complete Correspondence Between Thomas Jefferson and Abigail and John Adams*, edited by Lester J. Cappon (© 1959, The University of North Carolina Press, published for the Institute of Early American History and Culture, Williamsburg; and to the Trustees of the Boston Public Library for permission to quote from a letter of Abigail Adams. In addition, I gratefully acknowledge the willingness of the Library of Congress, Manuscript Division; the Historical Society of Pennsylvania; and the Smithsonian Institution to supply copies of manuscript letters.

I, as does everyone who writes on the Adamses, owe a vast debt to the past and present editors of the Adams Papers: L. H. Butterfield, Marc Friedlaender, Robert J. Taylor, Richard Alan Ryerson, and Celeste Walker. I am grateful for the services of John D. Cushing of the Massachusetts Historical Society, Paul T. Heffron of the Library of Congress, and William L. Joyce of the American Antiquarian Society. H. Hobart Holly of the Quincy Historical Society provided expert guidance on the local history of Weymouth, Braintree, and Quincy. I profited from suggestions on the many medical problems of Abigail Adams by Paul Duffy and the late Edgar J. Geist, Jr., M.D.

Oscar Handlin possesses the rare editorial skill of improving a manuscript while respecting the integrity of an author's work. Nearly every page of this book has benefited from his diligent employment of that skill. In preparing the revision I have also benefited from insightful reviews of the first edition by: Cynthia A. Kierner, University of North Carolina, Charlotte; Patricia L. Meadow, Louisiana State University, Shreveport; Kerby Miller, University of Missouri, Columbia; and Robert A. Trennert, Arizona State University.

The late Marian Wilson, an editorial associate of Oakland University, made an important contribution to every stage of the first edition of this book. Abigail Adams would have much admired Mrs. Wilson's devotion to excellence.

My wife, Eleanor Emery Akers, has tolerated and supported my long "affair" with Abigail Adams.

Index